Mary A. Walker

Old Tracks and New Landmarks

Wayside Sketches in Crete, Macedonia, Mitylene, etc.

Mary A. Walker

Old Tracks and New Landmarks
Wayside Sketches in Crete, Macedonia, Mitylene, etc.

ISBN/EAN: 9783337015053

Printed in Europe, USA, Canada, Australia, Japan

Cover: Foto ©Andreas Hilbeck / pixelio.de

More available books at **www.hansebooks.com**

RUINED CISTERNS AT ISMIDT.

Frontispiece.

OLD TRACKS
AND NEW LANDMARKS

Wayside Sketches in Crete, Macedonia, Mitylene, etc.

BY

MARY A. WALKER

AUTHOR OF
'THROUGH MACEDONIA,' 'EASTERN LIFE AND SCENERY,' 'UNTRODDEN PATHS IN ROUMANIA,' ETC.

REPUTED BURIAL-PLACE OF HANNIBAL.

WITH ILLUSTRATIONS

LONDON
RICHARD BENTLEY AND SON
Publishers in Ordinary to Her Majesty
1897

[*All rights reserved*]

To

H. E.,

THE BARONESS DE CALICE,

TO WHOSE

KINDLY SYMPATHY WITH MY WORK AND WANDERINGS

I OWE MUCH OF THE HAPPINESS OF MY LIFE IN THE EAST,

THESE RAMBLING SKETCHES

ARE

RESPECTFULLY AND VERY LOVINGLY OFFERED.

August, 1897.

PREFACE.

Extract from a letter to the Author from Sir Donald Mackenzie Wallace.

DEAR MRS. WALKER,

In general terms I may say that your simple, unpretentious, graphic sketches are quite charming, just what I expected, from my recollection of previous work of yours. Though I have not visited all the places which you so graphically describe, my long residence in Turkey enables me to form a good general estimate of the accuracy of your descriptions; and I do not hesitate to say that those light and airy sketches convey more of the local colouring and the subtle local aroma—if I may be allowed to use such an expression—than any of the numerous books of travel in Turkey which I have read. They have nothing of the guide-book about them, and they might perhaps be described as mere impressions; but they have none of the tantalizing vagueness of the so-called impressionist school. Still less are they the impressions of the globe-trotter. They are, in fact, in spite of this apparent sketchiness, very carefully drawn little pictures by one who has a keen, practised eye for picturesque little details and an intimate knowledge not only of the past history of the country, but also of the character and customs of the various sections of the population, the keenness of observation and accuracy of knowledge being always tempered by that kindly sympathy which helps an outsider to see things from the inside.

You are quite at liberty to make any use you think fit of this letter, for it is written by me, not as a friend, but as an impartial critic.

Yours very truly,

DONALD MACKENZIE WALLACE.

LONDON,
September 21, 1897.

CONTENTS.

AN OLD PORTFOLIO - - - - - - 1

HAÏDAR PASHA IN 1857.

A peaceful scene—The iron doorway and the holy well—In the shade of the plane-trees—The bay of Kadikeuy—Stamboul from Asia as seen forty years ago - - - 3

ON THE ROAD TO ISMIDT, 1880.

Railway encroachments — An unexplored passage — The 'tchousch' vines of Kizil Toprak—Site of a summer palace of Justinian—Kaïsch Dagh—Bostandji Keupru and Byzantine ruins — Touzla—Guebsé — The mosque and the 'mezarlik'—A frugal repast—Two sinless cats—Eski Hissar, ruined palace and fortress—Heréké—Beautiful scenery of the Gulf of Ismidt—Mineral baths founded by St. Helena - - - - - - - 7

ISMIDT.

The fishing nets—The 'tcharshi'—Clotted cream—Pumpkins—The cemetery—A ruined cistern—Lukium—Yokkah—An ancient fountain—Our guide's guide—Old walls of Nicomedia—Eminé Hanum and her Imâm—A happy marriage—'Tchórba · morba'— Our sailors' graves — Ruins of the time of Diocletian—St. Pantaleïmon—The value of a cock's crow - - - - - - - - 20

CONTENTS

FROM ISMIDT TO ANGORA.

Unhealthy marshes and water-supply—Pliny's preoccupations —Refugees, good and evil—The lake of Sabandja—Justinian's bridge—In Œunu and its rock caverns—Eski Shehir —Hotel Gaëtano - - · - · - 37

THE PLAINS OF ANGORA.

Spring colouring—Storks—Flocks of milk-white kids—Field flowers—A village of mud huts—Approach to Angora · 47

ANGORA.

Comfortable lodging—Vandalism—The Queen's birthday— 'Tiftik' and the Angora goats—The weight of a key— Temple of 'The God Augustus and of The Goddess Rome'—A monumental doorway—The Latin inscription— Discovery of the Greek text—Ruthless destruction—The Téké of Hadji Baïram—Column of Julian the Apostate— Church of St. Clement—Monastery of Vauk—A Byzantine church—A baptismal font—Cupids or angels?—Afternoon tea and the charm of civilization—In the fortress—Vast panorama—The plain of Tchibouk Abad—Djin Kalé— A marble lion—The Phrygian lion of Kalaba—Hideous defacement of the Seldjukian fortress—Inscriptions and sculptured fragments—Some remains of Doryleum - - 51

HISTORY OF ANCYRA.

Legendary origin — Derivation of the name—The great temple—St. Paul—St. Clement—One of the first cities of Asia Minor—Conquered by Heraclius—Pillaged by Haroun-al-Rashid—The Seldjuk dynasty—Immense amount of antiquarian fragments · · - · - 76

SUMMER DAYS IN CHALCEDON, 1865.

Moda Bournou—A Montenegrin princess—A garden—The terebinth walk—Happy home-life—Nicodemus and his peculiar views—Fanaraki, its ruins and its cypresses—A neglected vineyard—Funereal vases : their destiny—Broken bits · - · - - · - 80

CONTENTS

UNDER THE OAKS AT MERDIVENKEUY.

The bullock araba—Story of Don Andrea—Emotional travelling—A shady glade—Turkish open-air life—The cholera—A fearful visitation—The footsteps in the night—At Haskeuy—Moslem piety—Revived hope—The return of the birds - 99

BROUSSA IN 1866.

Seen from the Hôtel Loschi—The trysting-tree—A Jewish patriarch—Hadjis and zeïbeks—A picturesque group—The sacrifice of sheep - - - - - - 116

THE KEBAB SHOP.

The road through the bazaars—Wayfarers—Camels—A larded Sauton—The art of cooking kebabs - - - - 122

BROUSSA IN 1886.

The cradle of the Ottoman race—Genuine Osmanlis—View from the castle hill—Mountain summits—Forest-clad slopes—Bounar Bashi—Tékés and venerated tombs—The mosque of Bajazet - - - - - - 126

BROUSSA IN 1896.

Changes, useful but deplorable—Rail from Mondania—Road to Tchekirghé—Gheïk Deré—The new college - - 131

IN MACEDONIA.

CAVALLA.

Striking situation—Fortifications and the Roman aqueduct—The Via Egnatia—The road to Philippi—Dreams: the Roman eagle and the Pilgrim's staff - - - 134

PELLA.

A brilliant cavalcade—The Plain of Vardar—The khan of Pella—Shade and rest—Remains of a Roman reservoir—Tumuli—Rough lodgings—The khandji—Travelling resources - - - - - - - 138

VODENA.

At the Archbishop's palace—A courteous and anxious host —Exquisite situation of Vodena—Cascades—Luxuriant foliage - - - - - - - 146

OCHRIDA.

Churches founded by Justinian—The Metropolitan church— Interesting inscription—Pauselinos of Thessalonica—The Albanian mountains—Lake of Ochrida—Our cavalcade— Costumes—A dignified approach—Monastery of St. Naûm —Welcoming peals—Elaborate preparations for famished travellers—Foundation of the monastery—The 'Mission of Seven'—Cyril and Methodius—Conversion of King Bogaris —Tomb of St. Clement—A cure for lunatics—Source of the Black Drin—Fishing at Struga—Salmon-trout—The fur trade—Eminé Hanum and her Albanian visitor - - 152

RECOLLECTIONS OF MITYLENE.

Approach to Mitylene—Difficult disembarkation—Beautiful scenery—The chair of Potamon—Remains of Temple of Apollo—Fragments of antiquity—Capitals—Mosaic pavements—May-day garlands—The castle—Ancient cistern— Climate of Mitylene—Prosperity of the inhabitants— Gratuitous education—Brisk trade—Testing the wine and oilskins—The market—Open-air manufactures—'Rhigani' —Beauty and costume of the Mityleniotes—The helmet of Minerva—Erinna, her poems and early death - - 167

THE HARBOUR OF THE OLIVES.

On the road to Hiéra—Goats and their favourite food— Beautiful view towards Pergamos and Smyrna—The mineral springs of Kendros—Volcanic nature of the island—The hot springs of Polichniti - - - - - - 186

THERMI, THE GREAT CYPRESS AND THE RUINED AQUEDUCT.

A cargo boat—The baths—An uncanny group of bathers— Fragments of sculpture and inscriptions—Mineral qualities of the water—The giant cypress-tree—Superstitions—The ruined aqueduct—A splendid Roman work—Destruction by earthquake and vandalism—Water-towers - - - 191

MOLIVO AND PETRA.

What waiting means—Up the face of a precipice—Midnight disturbance and hospitality—The Genoese castle—Volcanic rocks—Lovely scene from the old bridge—Methymna in mythological times—Lesbian wine—Its treatment—On the road to Petra—An ancient subterranean way—The church on the rock—Arms and emblems of the Gatelutzi family—A deep well—An early (!) steamer—Waiting—Hospitality and its possible reward—'The boat! the boat!' - - 198

IN CRETE.

THE AKROTIRI.

A sandy road — Africa Minor — Aromatic plants — The 'lavdanum'— View from above Khalépa — A fortified Venetian house—Difficult climbing—Perfumed breezes—Sheïtanlik—Aghia Triadha—A ghastly closet—Travelling beehives—The fortified convent of St. John—Married priests — Beautiful wood-carving—A string of guides—Exquisite scenery—The cave of the bear—Cream cheese—Kathòlico—The stalactite cavern—Dangerous progress—Legend of the rock chapel of St. Elias · - - 209

GHONIA.

With Reouf Pasha in the konak—Elaborate preparations for an excursion—The leper village—Alikianos—An orange grove—Unhealthy situation—A polite caïmakam—Unrestful rest—Hospitality at Ghonia—Church pictures and wood-carving—Cretan notions—Reouf Pasha a beneficent Vali—Platània—The value of a 'havouz'—Silk-winding—Parkke olive grounds—The arsenal—The Arab village—Subcts for the pencil - · - - - - 233

THE DANUBE AND THE BOSPHORUS.

THE DANUBE ROUTE: WESTWARDS, 1872.

Varna an open roadstead—Tribulations—Pretty scenery—Rustchuk — The Danube — The slow service on the *Szechényi* — The dreary Wallachian shore — Fellow -

passengers—The cadi and his party—A Wallachian family—The benefits of idleness—Dinners and 'dàbls'—Increasing animation—Trajan's Bridge—The sturgeon of Turno-Severin—The old Roman road—The Iron Gates—Orsova—Costume of Wallachian women—Sublime scenery—Illusions—Semendria—Belgrade—Hungarian ladies—A blaze of fashion—The black mills—Buda-Pesth—Hôtel Hungaria—The Coronation mound—The Blocksberg—A mislaid trunk and Hungarian courtesy—Vienna—Improvements—Mölk—Passau—The meeting of the waters—The river Maine—Reposeful scenery—The Rhine—Transformations—Vexation of spirit—Fine situation of Huy—Money changing—Paris—Bewilderments—Ruined monuments—Nôtre Dame—Relics—Senseless destruction round Paris—Village life—The Uhlan and Père Étienne—A sick Bavarian—German moderation—In England—London—The Underground—Wealth and poverty—An East London train—The heart of the world - - - 251

IN MID-WINTER, FROM VIENNA TO GALATZ.

Companions in the 'Damen Coupé'—Alone—Frozen windows—The expiring lamp—Nervous terrors—Compassionate guards—Cracow—Travelling wraps for Continentals—Galicia—Pretty scenery—Czernovitz—Suczava—Romàn—Barboshi—'Capi di Bové,' a Roman encampment—Galatz - - - - - - - - 317

OUR BEAUTIFUL WATERWAY: BOSPHORUS VIGNETTES.

Tourists and their labours—The cabin of a 'zig-zag'—A central Asian group—The scala of Cabatasch—Dolma Bagtché—Beshiktash and the tomb of Barbarossa—Tcheraghān—An evil omen—Ortakeuy—The yali of A——Sultana—Anecdote—The Tulip Kiosk: its origin—Palaces and gardens of the Khedive—Païdos at Kavak—The ruined castle—'Dalyans'—The yali of Fuad Pasha—Fête in the harem—The Princess Halim—From a yali at Candilli—A floating market—Looking towards Europe—A devastated hillside—The towers of Roumeli—Ahmed Vefyk Pasha—The American College—The téké of the Bektashies—Their cemetery - - - - - - - 331

LIST OF ILLUSTRATIONS.

RUINED CISTERNS AT ISMIDT		*Frontispiece*
ENTRANCE TO HOLY FOUNTAIN IN 1857		*To face p.* 2
HAÏDAR PASHA IN 1857		,, 4
OLD HOUSE, ISMIDT		,, 28
FANARAKI		,, 84
MODA BOURNOU		,, 92
AT MERDIVENKEUY		,, 106
OLD ROMAN BRIDGE, BROUSSA		,, 116
SURIDJI, BROUSSA		,, 132
CAVALLA		,, 134
VODENA		,, 148
OCHRIDA		,, 152
MONASTERY OF ST. NAÛM		,, 156
RUINED FORT, MITYLENE		,, 168
KENDROS: THE HARBOUR OF THE OLIVES		,, 188
RUINED AQUEDUCT, MITYLENE		,, 194
CASTLE OF MOLIVO		,, 200
CANEA FROM KHALÉPA		,, 212
RUINS OF KATHÒLICO, AKROTIRI		,, 226
OUTER HARBOUR OF CANEA		,, 232
RUINED CHURCH ABOVE PERIVOGLIA		,, 236
WITHIN THE MONASTERY, GHONIA		,, 240
AMONG THE HUTS, CANEA		,, 250
THE BOSPHORUS, FROM ABOVE KURFESS		,, 330
ROUMELI HISSAR		,, 356

OLD TRACKS
AND NEW LANDMARKS

———•———

AN OLD PORTFOLIO.

A MASS of little sketches in an old portfolio, taken in many lands and at varying intervals during a long lifetime. The earliest are feeble records of youthful delight in the first view of real mountain scenery, gained when travelling— not, as yet, a railway rush—was carried on by the lumbering stage-coach or diligence, by the slow one-oared boat, by mule or horseback, and oftentimes on foot. How vividly the few slight touches recall every incident of those happy wanderings, which, as years rolled on, take one in memory to Normandy or Southern France; to many a wild scene in Macedonia and the Pindus Mountains; to Albania, Calabria, Crete, and Mytilene; to monasteries amongst the gorges of the Carpathians; to beautiful rivers — the Danube, the Moselle; to Athens, Broussa, and countless other interesting spots; until the last excursion, so recently undertaken with (dare I say it?) scarcely diminished pleasure and enthusiasm, shows ancient cities of Asia Minor—Nicomedia and Ancyra—as the aim and object of an old woman's exertions.

The old portfolio does not keep its records in order; they are mingled in rather bewildering confusion, but we can select those connected with the last little journey, for which the aid both of photography and the iron horse were gratefully, if somewhat regretfully, accepted. To start upon this line fittingly and thoroughly we must go back in time for nearly forty years.

Here is a small and apparently quite insignificant sketch, dated 1857, but it is probably the only existing record of any construction connected with the celebrated Church of St. Euphemia, which was utterly destroyed more than four centuries ago.

ENTRANCE TO HOLY FOUNTAIN IN 1857.

HAÏDAR PASHA IN 1857.

IT is a scene of calm and peaceful beauty—peaceful then, although the throb and hurry of the Crimean War had but so recently subsided, leaving its sad memorials beneath the grass and flowers of the beautiful Scutari burial-ground.

The place is Haïdar Pasha, a projecting point of land on the Asiatic shore of the Bosphorus, forming one side of the bay of old Chalcedon (now Kadikeuy): a breezy spot, shaded by two groups of noble Oriental planes; in the foreground some old masonry, with a rough descent, leading, by an iron doorway, into a small, dark, vaulted chamber, in which is found an 'ayasma,' or holy well, that was once enclosed in the precincts of the great Church of St. Euphemia, the scene of the celebrated Council of Chalcedon.

In the cool shade of the spreading plane-trees,

a few loungers sip their tiny cups of coffee and smoke the dreamy narghilé or tchibouk. Through an opening one can see another mass of stone or marble close to the shore ; it may possibly also have been connected with the ancient church. Between the two groups of plane-trees the blue waters of the bay ripple with diamond sparkles, as a gentle breeze slightly stirs the surface, and further back the point of Kadikeuy, at that time little more than a considerable village, shows some brown and reddish houses above the primitive little steamer *Scala*. Beyond the point the islets of Plati and Oxïea, and in the distance the green masses of the mountain chain bordering the Gulf of Ismidt, with evanescent glimpses of the snowy crest of Mount Olympus.

The view of Stamboul, taken from this point at that long past time, may seem to a casual observer to show the well-known outline of minarets and towers and encircling walls, but to the few who now remember the ancient city as it was nearly forty years ago, some changes will be evident. The towers of the Seraglio and of Galata are crowned with their pointed extinguisher-shaped summits. The extreme end of

HAÏDAR PASHA IN 1857.

the Seraglio gardens shows the picturesque group of pavilions forming the Winter Palace (burnt in 1865). The sea walls, though crumbling, are continuous, and have not yet yielded to the encroachments of the railway line. On the rising ground to the right the old wooden konak, given by the Sultan Abdul Medjid to Admiral Slade, stands empty and forlorn, looking down upon a broken minaret amidst a cluster of small cafés and fishermen's huts.

Turning landwards, the rough road passes a marble fountain, also shaded by plane-trees, then wanders across a broad meadow glowing with wild flowers and tall, waving grasses towards a group of lofty cypresses mingled with softer masses of green foliage. A bullock araba is winding slowly along towards a cluster of brown wooden houses, and a small mosque with its white minaret; the background—the vineyards and gardens of Tchamlidja—completes the calm and peaceful picture.

The hill rising on the left hand of the valley is the supposed site of the ancient Church of St. Euphemia, built by Constantine on the site of a temple of Apollo. After the fall of Constantinople the church was destroyed, and the materials used in the building of the Solimanyeh, the most beautiful of the mosques in Stamboul that had not been a Christian church.

ON THE ROAD TO ISMIDT, 1880.

YEARS have rolled by, bringing their inevitable changes. We are now in 1880. The calm beauty of the scene has vanished, and in its place the noise and bustle of a small, though as yet insignificant, railway-station has enclosed in its grim precincts the holy well of St. Euphemia. It is not destroyed (an 'ayasma,' or holy fountain, is never in this country destroyed), but it is lost to view somewhere in the lower parts of the straggling building. The beautiful plane-trees have been cleared off the ground; the flowery pasture is gray and unsightly with dusty railway-sheds; small, unpicturesque houses cover the rising ground; and as the train glides slowly through a short cutting, we can see on the right bank that a passage or tunnel has been cut through obliquely. This passage, about the height of a man, is narrow and vaulted with tiles apparently thrust in roughly from beneath. It takes the direction of the ancient city (Chalcedon), and not that towards the sea, as would be the case with a drain or watercourse, and there seems little room to doubt that this must be the subterranean passage through which the Persians in the seventh century passed from their camp on the rising ground of Haïdar Pasha to the market-place of Chalcedon, which they were besieging, and which they thus took by surprise.

When the works for this line of railway were begun, many important fragments of antiquity were brought to light. Some of these remained for several years on a piece of neglected ground near the station, others were broken up or dispersed; but this particular vaulted channel escaped notice, and, in the belief of the writer, has never been sufficiently examined.

The line passes along a track rich in pastoral beauty: in vast vineyards yielding the far-famed 'tchousch' grapes of Kizil Toprak, with splendid orchards bearing the equally esteemed cherries; villas and country houses surrounded by their glowing gardens on a land teeming with historical remembrances. Now it is the ancient chapel of St. John Chrysostom, with its holy well under the shade of giant plane-trees; next the beautiful cypress-covered headland of Fanaraki, where many a piece of sculptured marble, handfuls of mosaic cubes, fragments of ancient vases, are found in the cliff sides or on the shore beneath the spot where once stood a summer palace of Justinian. Then the bright chaplet of the Princes' Islands, sparkling with their gay villas and luxuriant gardens, on the right hand of the line; while the inner side shows a wild upland leading amongst rocks and brambles and low shrubs to the summit of Kaïsch Dagh (Mount Auxentius), the highest point in the neighbourhood of Constantinople, and the last of a line of fire-beacons that stretched across Bithynia to the capital, communicating with a lighthouse on the Seraglio point. Mosaic tesseræ and other fragments may still be found on the summit, where, under the Greek Empire, a church and a celebrated monastery existed. Constantius calls this the Convent of the Holy Apostles, and says that two ascetics from the community became Patriarchs of Constantinople. The convent, destroyed by the Latins, was rebuilt by Michael Paleologos, and re-dedicated to St. Michael.

We pass an interesting old bridge—Bostandji Keupru—which recalls the fact that, until lately, considerable Byzantine ruins existed on this spot. Belisarius, Justinian's famous general, possessed much land in this neighbourhood. The whole of this shore of the gulf was a favourite summer resort of wealthy Byzantine nobles.

We are now passing a rock-strewn eminence, Maltépé (Treasure Hill), on which stood a summer palace of the emperors, and many legends exist of the supposed riches lying buried somewhere beneath the surface, and guarded by formidable ' djins.'

As the train, skirting the shore, advances towards the head of the gulf the scenery improves in beauty. On the land side thickets and woodland glades, showing tufts of heath, cistus, and myrtle, with sprinkled groups of ilex, are varied by some marshy lands, where mighty reeds wave their feathery blossoms majestically ; on the other side small islets covered with pine-trees are mirrored in the clear blue water.

The little station of Touzla stands in a grove

of oaks—a pretty sylvan scene, dotted with white tents, and leading on to great stretches of tobacco in full bloom. And so—on and on—till the station and viaduct of Guebsé form the limit of a short excursion.

From this point three objects of the highest interest are within reach — the burial-place of Hannibal on a lonely hilltop, marked by two gigantic cypress-trees ; the ruined castle near the shore ; and the little town of Guebsé (the ancient Lybissa), with its fine mosque, built in the reign of Soliman the Great ; its vast camel stables, where formerly the caravans of pilgrims rested on their way to Mecca, and the numerous fragments of antiquity scattered about the ' mezarlik,' or burial-ground.

Our little party on this occasion, between the three attractions, decided for the easiest and the most practicable. A few baggage-horses with native saddles awaited possible travellers to the town, which lies a mile or two inland, hidden from view of the station by a wooded slope ; so one of these, with his rider, was selected as guide; he was already laden with a heavy burden of raw meat for the same destination.

It was a glorious day of Indian summer, and our little party of four started bravely on foot, at first through a narrow lane, and past a wayside fountain under a group of plane-trees. On the summit of the little hill we pause to admire the view : the distant castle far below us on the right hand ; on the other side the lonely hilltop with its two sombre cypresses. We question the guide. 'There,' said he, unconsciously almost quoting Pliny, ' is the burial-place of a great man of the olden time—there, where you see the two cypresses.'

The people here are much more Oriental than those in Stamboul. The turban is the rule, and not the exception, and we felt, as we strolled on into the beautifully picturesque old town, as if we had drifted away from Western civilization.

The houses, delightfully irregular, draped with garlands of vine, with creamy-white, pale-blue, or maize-coloured upper stories and deep, overhanging eaves, are charming subjects for the pencil ; but the pavement also is irregular, and, in order to preserve one's enthusiasm, one must heroically ignore that fact.

We pass a large bath on our way to the great

mosque. Someone had constituted himself as guide, and, followed by a train of youngsters ready to rush in with information at the least hesitation of the leader, we are conducted into the shady, cool outer court. The inhabitants are justly proud of their fine 'djami.' It stands surrounded by considerable buildings—the 'khan' (resting-place for travellers), the 'medresseh' (upper school for students), the 'imaret' (a soup-kitchen for the poor), and the 'kitabhané' (library), which is above the principal gateway of the enclosure.

Our guide raised the door-curtain of the mosque, but, unwilling to disturb the group of twenty or thirty students seated on the ground, to whom an imâm, also on the ground, was reading, we did not advance, but could see that the interior was rich in inlaid marbles and Persian tiling, reminding one of the beautiful green mosque at Broussa; the 'mihrab,' the recess where the Koran is placed, is extremely rich in carving and decoration.

We wandered on into the burial-ground; fragments of old columns were lying about among the weeds and brambles, some of them serving as tombstones, with here and there some piece of engraved tablet, one large slab bearing a long Greek inscription; there is little doubt that this must have been the site of an ancient church. The principal object, however, of which the inhabitants seemed immensely proud, was a monumental structure, a dome raised on four arches, partly ruined, and covering two grass-grown graves in which reposed . . . the forty daughters of one Musulman lady, twenty in each grave; a wonderful family, but not without other examples in this part of Asia Minor, as I have heard a member of a well-known Smyrna family declare that a near ancestress was the proud mother of three-and-thirty children.

Once more in the market-place, we sat down on native 'iskemlé'—little wooden and straw stools—to await such refreshment as could be procured from the neighbouring café. It presently appeared, neatly arranged on a metal disc: dried salted meat in thin slices, country cheese, flaps of unleavened bread; but the central dish was the *pièce de résistance* of the feast—a large bowl of sardines, raw onions, and sliced tomatoes, well soaked with oil and vinegar. It was useless to be fastidious, and it was really very good of the people to give us anything at all, for they were in full Ramazan, fasting from dawn to sunset, fasting even from water and tobacco. This rigorous abstention is naturally trying to the temper, and we wondered to see the general public grouped around our little party, gazing benevolently, one of them even bringing a welcome addition in the form of a plate of magnificent black grapes.

The greater number of our rustic friends sat on their heels—a favourite attitude of rest in these countries. One serious-looking man, with a beautiful cat on either shoulder, seeing one of us taking a slight sketch of the mosque entrance, suggested the idea of drawings of his favourites. It was begun, but of course the man's head and shoulders formed part of the picture, and, being enlightened by the jokes of the lookers-on, the poor man, a devout follower of the Koran, would have risen from his heels and fled, to avoid the sin of having his likeness taken; but it was done. There was no help for it, and it was at least a great comfort to reflect that his cherished pets were not responsible.

Once more our little party is grouped in front of the rustic railway - station of Guebsé; this time with the intention of descending the valley to examine the ruins that appear to overhang the gulf, and which bear no name more distinctive than Eski Hissar (the Old Castle).

A roadway, winding amongst orchards and vineyards and fields of wheat, shaded by noble walnut and chestnut trees, leads downwards; one or two wayside fountains and the ruins of some ‘sou terazi’ (water-towers) bear testimony to the past importance of the now ruined and forgotten mass of buildings, that had evidently required costly works to carry the needful supply of water from the neighbouring hills.

At the end of the valley a short and rough climb brings us to the ruins, a vast enclosure of battlemented walls, strong towers and vaulted entrances, surrounding a massive square building, apparently of older date. On the side towards the water the fortifications take the form of a series of terraces reaching down to the shore.

The fine proportions of the central building, the height and size of the interior hall, the remains of columns of marble, porphyry and red granite, lying amidst the ruins, give the place the aspect of a princely residence rather than that of the keep of a fortress. The learned Patriarch Constantius says : 'Near to Pythia, Justinian built a palace'—Pythia or Polopythia being the ancient name of some mineral springs in the immediate vicinity used by Constantine, by Theodora, wife of Justinian, and by many other notable persons.

Von Hammer speaks of the place as having been a strong Byzantine fortress, and it is stated that it resisted the power of the Ottoman Turks until long after Nicomedia, Nicea, and the whole of the surrounding districts, had fallen into their hands.

In the present day the peasantry know absolutely nothing of its origin or history; but they have a liberal supply of dark and gruesome legends as connected with the crumbling walls.

Some authors think that it was at this place that Constantine the Great died ; others, that Heréké, the third station forwards towards Ismidt, must have been the scene of that important event, where the dying Emperor was baptized by Eusebius, Bishop of Nicomedia, and, 'retaining to the last the white garment of his baptism,' died in the year 337 A.D.

At the station of Heréké the train stops in front of the large imperial silk and velvet factory. On the opposite side the hill rises in a steep slope, where a ruined square tower and some remains of fortified walls appear amongst the thick forest growth. These ruins may be traced quite down to the shore, where also we find vestiges and remains of architecture that indicate the possible site of a palace. Von Hammer says the 'name Heréké may be a disfigured rendering of Ancyron, at which place, said to be in the neighbourhood of Nicomedia, Constantine had a villa.'

Beyond Heréké, the distances between the stations increase, as the scenery also increases in beauty. The opposite line of mountains—nearer now, as the gulf perceptibly narrows—are richly wooded almost to the summit, and throw their long shadows and reflections quite across the calm liquid mirror. The lilac tint is yielding to a soft purple shade that creeps upwards towards the still golden rock-crowned summits. Bright sparkles on the lower mountain slopes reveal, in the transparent haze rising from the still water, a solitary farm, or a little hamlet, or it may be the small lighthouse on the point of Dil-Iskelessy. We have long since passed the spot from whence (on the opposite shore) the baths founded by St. Helena, the mother of Constantine, can be pointed out. Valuable mineral waters, lying for centuries almost unknown, have lately sprung into notice, and are now much frequented.

The night has fallen, but we can discern through the gloom that the train is traversing vast fields of tobacco plantations; one of the stations, indeed, reminds us of the fact—it is Tutûn Ichiftlik (tobacco farm)—and it is evident that much forest growth has been cleared away in the interest of the 'weed.' And so, rolling on and on, a high hill, bright with the sparkling lights of a considerable town, rises on our left hand, and we know that we have reached the limit of our excursion, the station of Ismidt.

ISMIDT.

IT had been dark when we reached our resting-place, a small clean dwelling-house in which the host, Jorghios Bulgaropoulos, and his pretty young wife, Katinka, let three or four rooms, principally to ladies passing through Ismidt to or from the large American schools at Bagtchedjik on the mountain slope of the opposite shore of the gulf.

The morning light reveals a high wall shadowed by some fine lime-trees, the boundary of the extensive grounds of the arsenal; beneath, a narrow lane, leading towards the water, that glitters and sparkles with the fresh breeze; a little to the left hand a fragile wooden jetty, adorned for the time being with the wide-spreading, spider-like framework of the fishing nets.

Our first expedition was landwards, under the guidance of Jorghios (English rendering Georgy), or rather attended by him, for we soon realized that his views did not willingly embrace the idea of energetic exploration and hill climbing, but preferred a saunter, or, let us say, a stumble over the boulders and ruts that represent the roadway through the bazaars.

The 'tcharshi' is usually the chief point of interest in an Eastern city. Peasant costumes, unknown fruits and vegetables, uncouth wares of various kinds, may be best seen there; but in these bazaars of Ismidt there was little to be observed except the extraordinary size and quality of the leeks and cabbages, and the tempting snow-white rolls of caïmak, the clotted cream of the East, to be met with only in these lands and in Devonshire. Do the people of Devonshire know the origin of their clotted cream? Well, legends affirm that the knowledge of it reached them through the Phœnicians who came to the south-west coast of our barbaric isle in search of tin; but even here honest investigation gets a little confused, for the jealousy of Cornwall intervenes. 'Yes,' say the wise ones, 'it may be so, but *we* taught the Phœnicians!' Caïmak is a delicious product, only obtainable in perfection during the spring and autumn, when there is fresh pasturage for the cattle.

Our way led along the highroad, the old Roman road into the interior towards Bagdad. Bullock and buffalo carts were creaking and groaning their rough progress to and from the town, some with families of emigrants bound for the lands allotted to them by the Government, others conveying the manufactures of the district, principally in the form of reed matting; but the slow march was on this occasion enlivened by the irregular conduct of a baggage horse laden with the native pumpkin. Something had startled the much-enduring creature, and with a wild fling and clatter he rushed forward, regardless of consequences, scattering his golden-coloured burden about the ground. Eastern pumpkins have the form of ill-made water-bottles.

The road through the outskirts of the city eastwards passes beside a Turkish cemetery; the low boundary wall displays some fragments of exquisite ancient frieze-work inserted in the midst of the rough-hewn stones. The ground beyond rises steeply, a dark grove of venerable cypresses, moss-grown gravestones, rank weeds and wild blossoms. Here and there shafts of golden sunlight pierce the gloom to flash on a group of half-fallen turbaned head-stones, or to cast a bright glow on some old houses bordering a narrow pathway — old, dilapidated, wooden dwellings, their pale green or rose-coloured stucco all faded and stained and washed by sun and rain. It is beautiful, but the beauty of hopeless decay.

Still following the ancient roadway, we pass the mouth of one of those great drains mentioned by Texier—'great canals in which men may walk upright; they penetrate horizontally into the interior of the land, and show the remains of a vast and opulent city.'

We have reached the open country beyond the last straggling dwellings, and turn upwards on the left by a short roughly-marked track, where, amongst brambles, heather, and innumerable wild flowers, we find the flat tombstones of the Jewish burial-ground. Still upwards for a few steps, and we look down into the ruins of an immense cistern in massive brickwork, several columns supporting a vaulted roof.

Can this important work be in part due to Pliny, the energetic governor of Bithynia? His letters to Trajan show his great sympathy with the question of the water-supply of Nicomedia, and he proposes to utilize a certain watercourse, bringing it to the town by means of a *vaulted building*. Local tradition ascribes the work to Andronicus the Younger, but it may well have had a more remote origin.

The interior of these ancient cisterns received three coatings : first, of lime and cement ; second, a mixture of pounded charcoal and lime ; third, a stucco of great hardness formed of pounded stone, lime, and oil. This mixture (lukium) is mentioned in White's 'Constantinople,' with the remark that ' the impervious quality of it is so efficacious that, although some tanks are entirely beneath the earth, and thus perpetually exposed to outward infiltration as well as inward pressure, and undoubtedly coeval with the earliest Byzantine monarchs, yet there is no record of their requiring repair, or of their having ever leaked.'

When Orchan besieged Nicomedia he cut the water of this great cistern, in order to reduce the city.

The views from this point are extremely beautiful. On the one side the city rising in terraces, with its many-tinted houses, its gardens, minarets, groups of cypresses, crowned by the great Mosque of Orchan, built on the site of the ancient church, and seen in parts amidst masses of foliage. Ruins of the ancient battlemented wall strengthened by towers can be traced quite down the length of the hillside. On our left hand the gulf, where the lilac-tinted mountains, wreathed with fleecy cloudlets, cast long reflections in the still water; until they melt away in the verdant-looking but unhealthy marsh-lands at a short distance beyond the city.

We turn landwards, endeavouring to reach the summit of the hill, and our 'guide' having contrived to involve us in painful and perplexing difficulties, undignified scrambles over broken walls and through briary and muddy lanes, we find ourselves at length still wandering around the base of the steep ascent until our leader, having —to his and our intense relief—found a guide for himself, we finally take the right direction, and by a narrow pathway reach a cluster of little cottages on a terrace shaded by a grove of plane-trees. Some women, slightly veiled, are crouched on the ground, rolling out thin layers of paste into large flat cakes for drying; cut up in small strips, and once more dried, they are stored for winter use; this substance (yokkah), made of maize flour, is an excellent substitute for the rice used for pillau.

A few more windings along the steep hillside, and we reach an ancient fountain. The large slab at the back bears a double inscription, large letters partly covering smaller ones. Here some women are washing in an empty sarcophagus, their fluttering veils and faded antarys showing most picturesquely against the background of the fountain. Above we see an alcove-like vault of very ancient masonry, and beyond this, again, in the shadow of overhanging trees, a closed-up vaulted passage of immensely strong and very old construction.

With great benefit we have retained the services of our guide's 'guide,' and thus, still winding upwards, we find ourselves at one time outside the line of fortified walls, which, strengthened by towers at short distances apart, is considered as the boundary of ancient Nicomedia, the Greeks at a later period having descended to the foot of the hill near the water.

We re-enter the city over a mass of crumbled stone and rubbish, and reach at length the principal object of the day's expedition, the Mosque of Orchan. A fine Corinthian capital was lying in the road near the entrance gate, and within the court they show us a mass of marble or stone, supposed to have been a font of the old Christian church; it bears, they say, a long inscription, which is now covered and hidden from view by a wooden platform; a quantity of Indian corn, drying in the sun, covered the useful but uninteresting planks. We do not enter the mosque, but are told that within may be seen the remains of an altar. On this site stood the great church of Nicomedia, destroyed during the persecution of Christians under Diocletian.

Returning last evening to our little 'locanda,' I hear that an imâm had been there inquiring for me; after a moment's reflection, I understood the reason of the visit. A certain much-valued female 'halaïk,' a calpha, belonging to the household of my dear and respected friends, the family of A. Vefik Pasha, had been given in marriage a year or two previously to the imâm of a small mosque at Ismidt. I had intended inquiring after her, but, not knowing the address, the matter passed from my mind. I now remembered that, during our first walk in the suburbs leading us through the Turkish cemetery, I was startled by hearing my name spoken from one of those old wooden houses beside the road. I had thought it fancy, or, perhaps (influenced by the locality), djinns; it afterwards proved that Eminé Hanum had seen us pass, did not like to call out, but must have spoken the name in her surprise. She despatched her imâm to make inquiries. 'He had not known where to go,' he explained, when at last he discovered the right place; 'he had not slept all night; a worm was eating his heart with anxiety.'

I start the next morning with Jorghi. The imâm is on the watch for us near the entrance of his little mosque. Seeing our approach, without sign of recognition, he turns and walks on before; perhaps he did not care to greet a 'ghiaour' lady in the open street. But we are close to the house, where Eminé Hanum opens the door with a joyous and friendly welcome. She looks pale and sickly, and the house has a dilapidated appearance, rather disappointing,

OLD HOUSE, ISMIDT.

until, reaching the second floor, we find a pretty room, very nicely and completely furnished at the expense of the Pasha. Eminé also wears a neat new cotton dress, with a wadded jacket, a handsome diamond glitters on her finger, doubtless from the same old home where she had lived from earliest childhood, and for many years had nursed and tended the bedridden grandmother until her death.

She is delighted to hear of the old friends at Rouméli Hissar. 'I am pining,' she says, 'to see them all once more; I love them as if it were my own family; the Pasha and the Buyuk Hanum were to me as father and mother, the younger hanums like sisters; and little Fatma— I had nursed her from her birth. They will think it so ungrateful that we do not go to see them, but we cannot afford the double journey.' She entreats me to explain this to the family on my return.

We are sitting on the divan, sipping, first, delicious coffee; afterwards sherbert made of pomegranate. There is a large tray of fruits, and in his great hospitality the imâm (his name is Hafuz Emin) cracks walnuts, peels apples, cuts little pieces ready, and enters on the subject of his grievance—for he has a grievance, poor man !—and is at this moment suffering from a very unjust deprivation of his office of imâm of the small mosque near the market, Erdjiler Djami, although the imâmlik has been in his family for some generations. He shows us all the firmans, and explains his trouble. A year or two back, having been taken for a soldier, during a time of war, he had been necessarily replaced in his religious functions; and, on his return, could not regain his position, and has been obliged for the present to resign himself to the inferior post of muezzin ; but the usurping imâm is often ill, and Hafuz Emin Effendi is obliged to take the duties. I am urgently requested to bring this matter to the notice of the Pasha ; and I may now add that the worthy man, after some delay, was reinstated in his proper office. Then he passed on to the subject of his marriage, relating how, some years since, A. Vefik Pasha, then Governor of Broussa, stopped at Ismidt on a Friday and went to *his* mosque ; the old father of Hafuz Emin preached ; he himself read. The Pasha was much pleased, and gave liberal presents ;

and long afterwards, when seeking for a good husband for the trusty calpha (a superintendent), he remembered this man, now no longer very young, and they were married. 'We live,' said the imâm, 'in perfect harmony; there is never one unkind word. Before my marriage I used to suffer from fever, but she has taken such care of me, giving me "tchorba-morba" (broth and similar things), that I am now quite well and strong.'

This little incident of Turkish life amongst the humbler classes, literally repeated word for word; the status of a 'slave' in respectable old-fashioned families, and the happy if humble home of Eminé and her imâm, may seem to the Western mind unreal, but it is, nevertheless, an experience not unusual amongst those whose daily lives are little known beyond the limits of their quarter or village.

The term 'tchorba (broth) morba' can hardly be understood by strangers; it is a curious use of the letter *m* in place of the first letter or letters of the word, to indicate 'the like'; it is scarcely, I think, in the dictionary. Thus, a person may speak of a pen, 'calem,' and say 'calem malem,' meaning a pen and such like things; 'carotta, marotta' (carrots and such); 'colaï (easy), colaï molaï' ('Easy, do you say? What is that to me?'), etc.

Towards evening we start for a visit to the church and monastery of St. Pantaleïmon, at about half an hour's distance on the western side of the city. We have taken our guide — who cannot this time mistake his way—and stroll along the highroad, past a miserably forlorn and dilapidated shanty; an old board hanging amid the faded tangles of creeping plants announces it as 'The Duke of Wellington Public-house, Coffee Room and Luncheon Bar.' It is a relic of the sojourn of the British Fleet in the Gulf of Ismidt. A sadder and more touching memorial is found under the beautiful grove of plane-trees—to the left of the road—that shade the Christian cemetery, within which a small enclosure contains the graves of our English sailors from the ships of war; and one pathetic headstone records the names of those who perished by an explosion on board the *Thunderer*.

Before regaining the highroad, Jorghi took us across a large uncultivated extent of ground reaching as far as the railway works; for a considerable distance rough grass-grown mounds crop up irregularly; on nearer approach, they prove to be remains of ancient and very solid masonry. This spot has been mentioned by one author as the site of the palace of Diocletian; local tradition calls it the site of the great monastery of St. Nicholas, and the scene of the fearful massacre of Christians in the beginning of the fourth century, when, at Easter time, 20,000 persons were assembled, who, refusing to offer sacrifice to the heathen gods, were burnt within the vast enclosure of the monastery.

It is believed by the natives that much treasure and antiquarian remains are buried beneath these mounds, and they tell of subterranean passages now closed. These may be mythical, but the large fragments of sculptured marble lying among the tall thistles, a Corinthian capital and broken shafts of columns, some of them inserted in the courses of brickwork, an overturned pedestal with the inscription, 'Avrilios ernothoro Valerios Ercolius'; the extent of ruined vaults, into some of which we penetrated and made careful sketches, all seem to verify the opinion that this may have been the site, not of a palace, but of the ill-fated monastery.

Pursuing our road towards St. Pantaleïmon, we remark that in the rough, irregular paving many fragments of sculptured marble seem to have been turned to practically ignominious use. In a small field belonging to this monastery lies a white marble sarcophagus with a Latin inscription, the tomb of Valerio. ('Marcia raised this monument to Valerius Vincentius, Accountant of the Guards, my sweetest husband with whom I lived six years.') The cover of this sarcophagus serves as a trough for the fountain opposite the entrance gate of the monastery; but before reaching it we are taken to a grassy platform, beneath an ancient olive-tree. It was here that St. Pantaleïmon, after suffering fearful tortures, was put to death in the time of Murad I.* This Ottoman prince, on his road to Bagdad, passing by Nicomedia, sees the great and beautiful monastery; and, through a misunderstanding (to quote from a local history), orders the destruction of the community and of the building.

* On this grassy platform prayers are to this day offered on the anniversary of the martyrdom.

Soon afterwards, in a dream, a man, 'all in white,' reproaches him for his cruelty. Seized with fear, Murad summons his Grand Vizier, and gives orders to rebuild the monastery; it is done, and the Emir (still according to this legend), acting with truly Oriental 'fantasy,' proceeds to make compensation. A cock is placed on the highest point of the cupola; soldiers are stationed at regular distances all around. When the cock crowed, all the land as far as the sound could reach was to become the property of the monastery. A firman was also given freeing for ever from all State claims whatever goods should be brought to the monastic house. This firman holds good to this day; it is exhibited to each succeeding Sultan, and thus ratified and confirmed.

Many fragments of sculptured marble are inserted in the building and surroundings of the fountain; one, a female figure, is exquisitely graceful, and in the best style of art, although the slab has been, unfortunately, broken through.

The church is a modern building (on the ancient site), very garish and uninteresting, and much supported by Russian offerings, and a subsidy. It contains, however, some ancient inscriptions, doubtless from the former buildings; one of them states that 'Hierocles, at his own cost, raised this monument to Aurelia his wife, who lived with him decorously.'

The ancient chapel in the crypt is worth a visit; in the centre is placed the tomb of St. Pantaleïmon; the covering slab had been much hacked and defaced; formerly, colonnettes ornamented each corner, but the whole was now covered with draperies. Our guide slightly raised these on the left side of the tomb, and displayed two little white marble feet, beautifully sculptured, hanging over the side, as if just stepping down.

They say that when the tomb was opened a manuscript was found within, and they showed us ancient inscriptions on the stone flooring within the screen.

FROM ISMIDT TO ANGORA.

THE train leaving Ismidt for Eski Shehir and Angora glides gently away between the vegetable and fruit market on the left and a nicely planted roadway, backed by prosperous-looking stone houses. It might be concluded that the place had gained considerably by the extension of the line. The inhabitants, however, are not of that opinion. People now, they say, pass through instead of making Ismidt, as formerly, a central starting-point. I am making the excursion this time with two dear and sympathetic young friends, whose keen appreciation of natural beauty, and wise determination to make light of difficulties, offer the surest pledge of a prosperous and happy journey.

The suburbs of Ismidt on this side stretch in an untidy, picturesque, straggling manner along the base of the high hill down which the ruined walls and towers, revealed in glimpses amongst the luxuriant foliage, reach the lower slope, where they are lost in the orchards that I had once seen so rich and fruitful, before the refugees, in the time of the last war, cut them down for fuel, and left the beautiful hillside for many subsequent seasons bare.

We pass the corner of the Jews' burial-ground, and just perceive amongst the mass of flowering shrubs a part of the ruined ancient cistern, already mentioned as one of the most interesting remains of antiquity still left to Ismidt, and rolling onwards, pass the head of the gulf, where three or four small huts, used for the shooting of wild-fowl, rise out of the shallow water on piles. They are wonderfully picturesque, and so is the flowery but unhealthy plain upon which the line enters, for the much-dreaded marsh fever, so prevalent here, has caused more than one sad illness and death amongst our energetic British sportsmen. The drainage and utilization of these marshes has several times aroused the interest of monarchs and governors, always, as yet, without result. Pliny, the energetic pro-Consul of Bithynia, whose mind was greatly exercised on the subject of 'water-supply,' proposes, in a letter to the Emperor Trajan, a plan for joining the neighbouring Lake of Sabandja with the Gulf of Nicomedia. He speaks of an unfinished canal, cut by a former King of Bithynia, as an attempt at least to drain these marshes, and is himself enthusiastic in the hope of opening up this waterway—even, perhaps, as far as the Black Sea—by means of the river Sangarius. He earnestly begs that a competent authority may be sent to decide on the respective levels of the water. All these bright visions faded, notwithstanding the exceeding goodwill of Trajan. . . . But this was eighteen hundred years ago, and soon the network of junction lines which is spreading over this part of Asia Minor may possibly render the plan of a waterway of less value. The unhealthy marshlands, however, still remain, betrayed here and there by waving tufts of tall flowering reeds and clusters of beautiful yellow iris starring the soft expanse with gold. The broad valley is bounded by richly-wooded hills and finely-cultivated slopes, with many an emerald patch of young corn or pasture at their base. The railway line runs, for a considerable distance, parallel

with the ancient caravan road into the interior,
and we pass long, slow trains of buffalo and
bullock-carts, with their families of refugees, still
wandering on towards the settlements on vacant
lands granted to them by the Government. Some
of these tribes, such as the Pomaks from Bulgaria, the Tartars from the Dobrudja, have
brought with them habits of industry and cultivation; others—the Circassians and the Lazes—
have brought misfortune, pillage, and devastation
to the land that welcomed them so hospitably,
and we soon had proof of the effects of their
wasteful extravagance in the widespread desolation of burnt and ruined forests on either side of
the line, before reaching the first station, Buyuk
Derbend, and beyond it for some distance towards
Ada Bazar. These clearings, with their blackened, weird-looking tree-stumps, appear to have
been sacrificed to little purpose. They look
squalid, stony, and neglected, but in parts where
the tall forest trees still remain, a wonderful
veiling of hanging draperies of long creepers,
reaching to the ground, give, the place quite a
tropical appearance. Many wild-looking Lazes
were lounging about the railway-station, with

their strange headgear and their picturesque look of irreclaimable brigands, but they were forgotten as the lovely scenery increased in interest.

For some time previously the valley had contracted; the mountain chain, richly wooded with dwarf oak, seemed closing in upon the green pastures, dashed with broad streaks of brilliant golden flowers, where innumerable storks marched majestically, or rose in their heavy flight from the terror of the rattling train, as the beautiful Lake of Sabàndja opened out into view—the more welcome, perhaps, because of the general scarcity of pieces of water. Tall flowering reeds wave gently in the breeze; cattle stand lazily ruminating amongst the gentle ripples of the margin; small boats rock dreamily, doubled by their reflections; a peasant's scarlet girdle adds a bright spot, as the train makes its stately progress between the tender blue of the lake and the dark forests rising abruptly on the other side, which now open out to show a Tcherkess village with its white minaret, dotted up the slope, among fields and copses until the station of Ada Bazar is reached.

Carriages are in waiting, and native carts with

white canvas awnings bordered and ornamented in bright red. It is principally from this station that travellers start to visit the celebrated bridge built by Justinian in the middle of the sixth century over the river Sangarius, which has long since changed its course. The bridge can first be perceived on the left of the line, above a rich mass of orchards and cultivation.

Leaving Ada Bazar, the first railway bridge over the Sakaria brings us into a grand wilderness of rock and foliage stretching high into the clouds: splendid mountain scenery, although, wherever sufficient space exists, the soil is richly cultivated. Then the mountains open out in grassy glades sprinkled with rustic thatched cottages. We pass the ruins of a khan half buried in ivy and creeping plants; magnificent walnut and chestnut trees, left to expand in full luxuriance of leafage; more cottages, whattled, plastered, and thatched; the hedges glow with roses—a region of sylvan glades. In one shady spot, beneath a tangle and blaze of wild azaleas creeping upwards into the forest, blossoming lilies float on pools of water.

At Geïveh a small village is rising near the station. The little town itself is seen climbing irregularly up the hillside on the left of the line beyond an old stone bridge built by Sultan Selim III. Not far from this, also on the left, the snowy crest of Olympus may be perceived towering above the nearer mountains. On the right the forest becomes once more thick and dense: gigantic masses and cascades of foliage above a blaze of poppies at its foot. The carriage-road, that in most parts runs beside us, passes by the base of a low earth cliff, where a curious round white spot looks as if some strong mineral water, gushing from the opening, fell in a tiny cascade to the roadway beneath.

After passing the station of Lefké, the line winds amongst stupendous mountain gorges, the forest-clothed summits and bold headlands of rock reminding one forcibly of the famous 'Desert' of the Grande Chartreuse; but we emerge at length from this sublime wilderness, to pause at the pretty little station of Vezir Khan, beautified by the draping of Virginia creeper and by its situation in a rich and fruitful valley, where the grand walnut-trees rear aloft their noble domes of foliage. The walnut wood of this part of Asia Minor is celebrated and much sought after.

The line here is carried along a considerable height. Several tunnels are passed; several bridges also, and viaducts winding amongst crags; here and there openings; glimpses of bright meadows; large herds of cattle feeding; buffaloes plunged to the head in muddy pools; sheep and goats and large flocks of snow-white kids; park-like slopes; a rustic mill turned by a rushing stream—the Kara Sou; and then again we are in a gorge between thickly-wooded, precipitous mountain walls, that leave scarcely room for the railway and a well-made carriage-road.

Throughout the day we have again passed long trains of refugee carts, with women and children, household goods and chattels, winding slowly along. Some of these trains, wending ponderously northwards, drawn by their heavy, ungainly buffaloes, are full of mighty rolls of reed matting.

The scenery increases in grandeur. At Bozyeuk, an important village, we have time to admire an ancient mosque, its dome strengthened by flying buttresses, the minaret a reddish-brown. The mosque is said to contain some good coloured tiles; there is also a khan, with two or three large stone houses.

The broad valley upon which we now enter is well cultivated, but the majestic forest-clad summits begin to recede and to lose their rich drapery, to give place to a thick carpeting of dwarf oak. The village of In Œunu, at some little distance from the station, is most picturesquely situated, climbing up irregularly towards a mighty rocky cliff, where may be plainly seen several cavern openings, some evidently natural, others perhaps artificially enlarged; for we are approaching those regions where the inhabitants have from time immemorial preferred to burrow in the earth for safety both from man and beast.

The next station, Tchukur Hissar (the Sunken Castle), points to some undiscovered interesting remains, and an old guide-book speaks of a curious and lofty mound. We only saw some splendid masses of light and shadow among the rocks, followed by a well-cultivated fertile plain sprinkled with villages. It was a pleasant but not exciting outlook, until our train rolled gently on, and stopped at sunset at the station of Eski Shehir, near the site of the ancient Doryleum.

In a small hotel quite near at hand—the Hotel Gaëtano, very clean, very comfortable, and exceedingly moderate in its charges—we found an excellent dinner and a calm and restful night, much needed after the heat and fatigue of the last ten hours.

THE PLAINS OF ANGORA.

FOR the traveller leaving Eski Shehir for Angora during the burning summer heats, when the crops have been gathered in, and the parched soil of the vast grazing lands shows through its scant covering of yellow dried-up grass, the long railway journey would be intolerably wearisome and monotonous; but, taken in the late spring-time, the aspect of this almost uninterrupted level, extending as far as Angora, possesses a wonderful fascination for those to whom the charm of Nature's colouring is really 'a joy for ever.'

On the left hand the great valley extends to the foot of a line of hills, forming a gigantic wall for nearly the entire distance. The summit of this boundary wall might have been levelled artificially; so perfectly even is it that only a thin streak of green appears to separate it from the background of dark blue mountain summits. The face of the cliff falls abruptly, scarped and lined as the sand or chalk or shale have shivered downwards; it looks as if at some unknown period of the earth's existence the plain had subsided, and left the giant barrier to mark its former level. In parts, towards the base, it is veined and accentuated by sudden irruptions of gray rock and grass-covered mounds, capped and crowned with dark bristling stony crests; they are generally gray, but occasionally a rough mass of dark red, veined with white, rears itself in the midst of the bright green corn. A tiny but busy little river, bearing the unpoetical name of the Pursak, ripples between alders and flowering reeds. Storks are everywhere; those which are not solemnly marching or heavily flying are perched in their monstrous nests on tops of hovels, or simply on a bare pole, as at Sarikeuy.

As we advance, the country becomes more varied in outline, and the mountain wall shows a thin line of forest above the chalk and sand; large flocks of milk-white kids dot the green surface of the broad pastures, and the beauty of colouring increases on the face of the distant cliffs, which show great splashes and streaks, now of intense orange, now of vivid carmine, now of dazzling white, and the rolling prairie beneath is painted with every imaginable tint of green, from freshest emerald to pale and tender olive, varied by long patches of violet vetch, with sprinkled tufts of yellow bloom, now a blaze of scarlet poppies, then of crimson thistles, and so on and on and on, until all is toned down and blended, and melted into the soft vaporous haze of distance.

The stations along the line are good and comfortable-looking, though wanting as yet the softening beauty of verandas and creeping plants, which are such a pleasant feature on the lines in Austria, Switzerland and elsewhere.

Before reaching Sindjankeni, the railway, leaving the level plain, enters a more rocky region. We pass a village of flat-roofed mud huts, very poor and miserable-looking, barren and treeless under the burning sun. The river is now upon our right hand, reflecting in its pools and depths great overhanging masses of brown crags. We are in a cutting through stupendous rocks; holes or caves in the great masses on either side; a flash through the pinky white chalk; another cutting; the gray mountain masses are covered with greenish moss, and then the village of Sindjankeni, another treeless, desolate collection of mud huts, from which we issue once more upon the many-tinted plain, bounded, as before, by its hill wall of white chalk, red earth, and dark green level.

A mountain rises in the distance above a nearer line of blue and lilac hills. We are drawing near to Angora. The hills are more chalky now, with many outbursts of gray rock, with holes and caverns. On the right hand several tunnels, on the left, large meadows with cattle, sheep and buffaloes; the land is dotted with white tents; beyond, the ancient city becomes visible, rising on three hills, the highest point crowned by the citadel of the old fortifications; a long white bridge in the foreground completes the picture. A few minutes later the train stops at the station, which is at a short distance from the base of the principal hill.

ANGORA.

No really comfortable hotel exists as yet at Angora, but through the kindness of Her Majesty's Consul, a very clean and suitable lodging has been prepared in the highest and best part of the city, opposite to the entrance of the enclosure of the citadel.

The daylight was fading when we arrived, after a very rough drive through the uneven, precipitous streets, and we had little opportunity for remarking anything except a very large and startlingly red object at a short distance in front of the windows. The next morning disclosed a thoroughly Oriental outlook, with its incongruities, its local colouring, and its varied costumes, not yet, one joyfully perceives, Europeanized. The incongruity proved to be a tower flanking the entrance gate of the castle; it has been recently painted a fine scarlet, standing out against the dazzling whitewash of the encircling wall; this enormity had been perpetrated by a former Vali, who, finding that the ancient citadel crowning the grand rocky summit was not, from a distance, sufficiently prominent and lively-looking, imagined this 'embellishment.'

The vandalism is distressing, but the purely Oriental character of the scene beneath the windows is charming. On one side a row of donkeys stand in the shadow of the overhanging upper story of one of those bewilderingly picturesque, latticed, tumble-down tenements that are the joy of the artist and the despair of sober-minded people. The donkeys are loaded with long rich swathes of fresh grass for sale; beside them, half embedded in the ground, a beautiful acanthus-leaf capital, reversed; near that, again, a hollow block (perhaps once also a reversed capital) in which a man is pounding a mass of gray-stone (pillon), much used in this country for washing purposes.

On the opposite side of the small irregular square a handsome-looking house is pointed out as the property of the Karaman Ogli family, a name so much connected with the earliest Ottoman records, that, were it not for the beautiful horses waiting at the gateway, with their well-appointed and most modern equipments, we might seem to have gone back six centuries.

In the front of our house the road winds steeply upwards towards the outer wall of the citadel; and, somewhat up the slope, we can see the groups collected at the fountain which yields the only supply of water for this part of the city; they are mostly women and girls; they pass to and fro, wrapped in their white garments like winding-sheets. All women here, Mussulman and Christian alike, wear the ghostly-looking wrapper of calico or muslin, edged with lace and very clean; it is pinned or held round the face, and covers nearly the entire person.

As we watch the animated scene near the fountain, and the silent, shrouded figures melting into the dim recesses of the archway leading into the citadel, we observe that many pause in groups on a rising ground a little withdrawn from the road, to gaze at the visitors, military and civilian, who are making their way upwards towards the

British Consulate, and we remember that to-day is May 24, the Queen's birthday. Presently, with a great clatter and rattle on the stony roadway, cavasses dash onwards, preceding the Vali, in a rich uniform covered with gold embroidery; he mounts a splendid Arab, much excited by the fitful blasts of the military band stationed in front of the Consulate, but the rider manages him beautifully, and preserves the dignity of his arrival; next, the Persian Consul, marked by his astrakan cap, also with much glitter and gold about his person, passes in a carriage, followed shortly by an Archbishop, some lesser dignitaries, and a few directors and clerks of the Ottoman Bank, the Tobacco Régie, and some other public establishments. The whole scene, with the attendant groups of sais, cavasses, and party-coloured retainers of all sorts, forms a brilliant spectacle; it glitters and flashes in the clear, pure air of this rocky summit, which has in itself some quality remarkably exhilarating and healthful. Angora, indeed, is looked upon as a health resort, and many invalids from the surrounding country are brought here to ensure their recovery.

It is a well-known fact that the air and water

of this district possess qualities which, combined, serve to produce the beautiful 'tiftik' (wool of the Angora goats), which combination of qualities exists absolutely in no other—as yet discovered—place, with the exception of the Cape of Good Hope, where the raising of those flocks is carried on to a great extent. The same influence acts in a more or less degree upon sheep and cats, and (presumably) upon most long-haired animals. The export of goats from the Vilayet of Angora is forbidden, now that it is almost too late to save this, the chief source of the wealth of the country.

Our first visit was paid to the ruins of the celebrated temple dedicated to 'The God Augustus and The Goddess Rome'; the temple on whose walls may still be deciphered the greater part of the famous Testamentum Ancyranum, carved in the marble, while the metal plates of the original inscription, of which this was a reproduction, perished long centuries ago in one of the overwhelming catastrophes that engulfed the power and the pride of ancient Rome. A facsimile of this most unique record is given in the great work 'La Galatie et la Bithynie' of Perrot and

Guillaume, from which I extract the title and the concluding lines.

The title declares this to be 'A Record of the Acts by which the Divine Augustus subjugated the Universe to the Power of the Roman People; of the Expenses incurred for the Republic and the People of Rome,' and states this to be 'an authentic copy of the record engraven at Rome on two tables of brass.' At the end we find, 'When I wrote this I was in my seventy-third year.'

Guided by our host, we pause at the Beilidiyeh (town-hall) to obtain the key. It is produced, after a short delay, by a policeman, accompanied by a second solemn official, presumably to relieve the first officer of the oppressive weight of an ordinary iron key! but the reason of the manœuvre became subsequently plain when it was suggested by our guide that nothing lower than a médjidié apiece could be offered to such responsible personages.

Before reaching the entrance gate we were joined by a Turkish gentleman, the secretary of the Vali, perhaps with a wish to visit the ancient ruin, possibly with the idea of ascertaining what might be the meaning of the rather unusual circumstance of the excursion of three lady visitors to Angora.

The old wooden doors opened upon a tangled mass of weeds and briars; some Turkish tombstones, mostly broken, neglected, uncared for, leaned forlornly to right and left amongst the rubbish, but in the centre towered a majestic object, a monumental doorway of white marble, the jambs and lintel preserving, almost entire, the exquisite carving in scroll and foliage, while parts of a band of rich frieze-work still ornamented the adjoining wall, and can be traced wherever time, neglect, or wilful destruction may have spared the upper portions of the monument. The very lofty proportions of this doorway doubtless account for the fact—not observed by Texier, but mentioned by Perrot, and obvious in the accompanying photograph—of the slight *narrowing* of the structure upwards; this magnificent entrance is called by the latter author 'one of the most complete of the rare ancient doorways that still remain.'

On the marble walls, at right angles, a great part of the celebrated Latin inscription may still be traced, the first part of it being on the left hand (as you face the doorway), the second part on the right; the Greek rendering of the Latin text was discovered, hidden by dwellings and stabling which, on the disappearance of the columns and porticos of the ancient temple, had been built against the outer wall of the great oblong hall into which you enter through the beautiful doorway. These buildings were mostly cleared away (temporarily) by Messrs. Perrot and Guillaume in 1861, and the Greek inscription photographed; it is now once more lost to view behind the sordid mud walls and sun-dried bricks that are permitted to deface this beautiful monument of ancient art and grandeur.

We passed onward into the great hall; here may be observed, on the right hand, the windows which were opened to give light to the interior when the pagan temple became a Christian church. Beyond these windows some traces of a partition wall still exist; and at the extreme end an addition to the building seems to have been made for the purposes of Christian worship; beneath this part some rude steps are said to lead into a crypt.

The wall forming the boundary of the hall on the right shows, in its marble blocks, the perfection of solid and careful workmanship, smoothed, fitted and put together without cement, but on the opposite side an enormous breach in the smooth surface recalls the fact that as late as 1834 a descendant of Hadji Baïram (whose Mosque and Téké adjoining the temple had, in the time of Sultan Soliman, already injured the beautiful monument), needing some marble for a bath in his country house, knocked down and carried off this large portion of wall.

Tradition affirms that bronze gates of corresponding richness and beauty to the stately gateway were carried off by Haroun al Rashid to adorn his palace at Bagdad; but this statement is not credited.

We left the enclosure, but paused—before the wooden doorway and the inexorable key should shut us out into the sordid lane—to admire the golden sunlight and breadth of shadow on the beautiful ruin towering above the weeds and brambles and neglected graves, and crowned at its apex by a gigantic stork's nest.

We were taken into the adjoining Téké of

Hadji Baïram; there was no mistaking the place, for the name in immense Arabic letters gleamed startlingly over the entrance through which you pass into a small courtyard. In a low, mean-looking building on the right hand side, the open door disclosed a length of stone wall covered with ancient inscriptions; some old men were performing their 'namaz' (prayer); and, respecting their devotions, we drew back, without discerning whether Greek or Latin were the language used and engraved on the stone or marble; I have since regretted the lost opportunity.

Not far from the Augusteum—the name by which the celebrated ruined temple is usually known—we were taken by many a tortuous, ill-paved lane towards the outskirts of the city, where, in an open irregular space, you come upon a tall column of a reddish colour. It is curiously formed of rings in high relief, and raised on a pedestal; the capital, of very inferior workmanship and style, displays shields held by acanthus leaves. On one side it is much broken away and defaced; it is needless to add that the storks could not resist such a tempting and secure position for a home, and an overpoweringly handsome mansion of twigs and brambles decorates the summit. The proportions of this column are singularly ungraceful, and indicate a period of decline in art. It is supposed to have been erected in honour of the Emperor Julian, who was received here, after his apostasy, with great honour and rejoicing by the heathen priesthood. He passed some time in this city.

Turning back towards the more populous quarters, in order to visit the ancient Byzantine Church of St. Clement, we could not but admire, so far as the excruciating nature of the broken paving-stones permitted, the picturesque look of the brick and wooden houses that overhang the turning, winding, narrow lanes of the old city: their projecting upper stories supported on heavy beams; their rows of small windows latticed in honeycomb pattern; here and there a trailing vine branch throwing flickering shadows on stone and woodwork; their deep eaves and general air of dilapidation; such 'bits'—ready-made pictures—may still be found in every Eastern city; but civilization, brought by steam and rail, is rapidly advancing on Angora with its inevitable accompaniment of brick and mortar tenements, perhaps even 'residential flats.' Happily these changes will principally affect for a long time to come the neighbourhood of the railway-station; and visitors may still take delight in the exceeding abundance of ancient remains to be found in Angora, in the upper parts of the city especially: fragments of Roman, Byzantine and Greek work, capitals and broken shafts of columns, bits of frieze worked into the mud walls, cornices, inscribed slabs, remnants of sculpture.

The old ruined Church of St. Clement stands in the enclosure of some private property, and we had ample time to admire a fine Corinthian capital, serving as a horse-block, before the proprietress, a Greek, made her appearance with a bunch of rusty keys. The wooden gate opened into a neglected, weedy yard, with some broken remnants of ancient marbles; but the most noticeable object was a small Angora cat, which fled at our approach. One looked at the flying mass of soft silky fur with interest, as this race of cats has almost disappeared from the city which is commonly supposed to be its native place.

The small Byzantine church, built of brick,

with pilasters in white marble, is in a most forlorn condition. The pilasters had originally displayed long crosses, but the transverse arms had been mutilated by Mussulman conquerors. Flanking the entrance doorway are the remains of two sculptured ankers; some imagine these to signify the origin of the name Ancyra.

It is supposed that St. Clement suffered martyrdom during the longest and most bitter, as it was the last, of the persecutions under Diocletian. He became the patron saint of the city, and soon after his death a great Council of the Church was held in Ancyra, to which came Bishops from all parts of Asia Minor, the President being the Bishop of Antioch. A large shapeless slab in the earthen floor is pointed out as covering the burial-place of the martyred Bishop.

In the afternoon a delightful drive took us into the country, turning at first towards the plain, in order to visit the ancient monastery of Vauk, belonging originally to a Greek community, now to the Armenians of the Gregorian rite. It stands pleasantly on a rising ground near a grove of fine old trees, a small stream rippling in the dip of the land. After some little delay, we are invited into the reception-room, where the Bishop, dignified and very polite, advances with a cordial welcome. A carriage had driven up in front of our own, and we found the occupants, one of them a Mussulman imâm, already seated on the broad divans. Conversation began in the usual slow, sententious manner of the East, the host and his guests no doubt inwardly wondering what could have brought three ladies to such an out-of-the-world place as Angora; but they were too polite to suggest the inquiry, and the stately speech and answer remained chiefly between the imâm and the Bishop. They discussed the virtues of a neighbouring mineral spring as a remedy for rheumatism; spoke of the weather and the prospects of the crops, carefully avoiding all the burning questions of the day; and we sat wondering when the coffee was likely to appear, when we should be invited to see the church, and, indeed, at last, whether we might not give up the investigation, retire politely and blandly, and once more find ourselves in the open carriage on our way to Mr. C——'s country house, rolling—more probably jolting—over the ruts and chasms of the road, but at least in the clear open country, enjoying the fresh thyme-scented breezes of that healthy locality. Release came at last, however, and, the coffee taken, the Bishop rose and proposed to show us the church.

A fine old Byzantine church, richly ornamented with the beautiful Kutaya tiling similar to that of the Yeshil Djami of Broussa. In the centre of the arched entrance into the church from the narthex, a curious stone is pointed out; it shows on the one side a heavily-carved cross, almost detached from the surrounding border; on the reverse side it forms a different emblem.

The modern frontal of the altar, richly embroidered in gold, is handsome, though not otherwise interesting; but a large baptismal font in a side chapel shows a curious and rather comical adaptation of what seems to have been a heathen altar to its present Christian uses. The frontal slab is of marble, beautifully sculptured with a group of dancing cupids, or bacchanalian children; now, slightly draped with wreaths of coloured leaves, they have been sobered down into attendant angels. In one of the windows they point out a 'yan tash' (burning stone), giving out a bright red glow; it is regarded as a wonder. We imagine it to be a thin slab of very transparent alabaster.

Outside the gate of the monastery a railing surrounding a burial enclosure attracted our attention. We were not invited to enter, a fact which I have since greatly regretted, on learning that not only does it contain the graves of some well-known English people who had died at Angora, but that in that spot may be seen many fragments of antique carving and inscriptions.

We are approaching a group of villas and country houses on a hill slope, at about an hour's distance from the city. At first strange jagged rocks seem to start up amidst the fields and thickets, a wild contrast to the soft foliage and stretches of cultivation. Gradually the rocky points subside, the leafy shade thickens, we are amongst gardens and orchards and winding lanes, and reach at length the end of our little excursion, the delightfully picturesque, vine-trellised summer retreat of our kind Consul and his charming young wife.

There is, perhaps, no contrast so keenly appreciated in these Eastern lands as the sudden change from the rough wildness of the scenery and people of the country, to the refinement and charm of cultivated intercourse, to be best met with among British Consuls in these far-away solitudes. It is delightfully satisfactory to unearth, or gaze upon, or sketch relics of ages lost in the dimness of legend and supposition; but that very modern afternoon tea-table, the kind intelligent father, the sweet and graceful hostess, and the lovely baby-boy, have left with us as pleasant a memory as any incident during our little expedition to Angora.

These country residences are endowed with a most abundant supply of water, each house having its own especial conduit from some source among the mountains. In this garden the never-ceasing trickle from the marble fountain amongst the rose-bushes added one other element of restful charm.

Returning to Angora by a different road in the cool of the after-glow, we notice once more the strangely weird masses of brown rock that burst upwards on all sides.

A cavass has come from the Consulate as our guide and escort into the enclosure of the fortress.

He leads us by a short but steep ascent, through the white gate of the citadel, into a labyrinth of tortuous lanes, becoming steeper still and steeper, and at length so narrow as almost to stifle our admiration for the beautiful lights and shadows of the old, tumbling, half-ruined houses, with their projecting upper stories, all mud and wood and plaster. We reach the last of the dwellings and come out upon a hillside, so rough with jagged rocks and fragments of stone and marble that until the summit is gained the surrounding scenery is unnoticed. It bursts upon our sight—a splendid panorama! Beneath and beyond the dwellings, mosques, and minarets of the lower town, the suburbs, with groups and clusters of foliage, stretch away towards the Armenian monastery and the broad and fertile plain, bounded by a line of high hills. Beyond that natural rampart lies the scene of the celebrated battle in 1402, between Beyezid Ilderim and Timour-Lenk (the lame Timour), commonly known as Tamerlane. The place is described as 'a smooth plain surrounded by mountains, looking like a vast circus;' it is now called the plain of Tchibouk Abad.

Near to the summit on which we are standing,

divided only by a deep and very narrow gorge, rises a conical-shaped hill, bearing on its point between two crags a small edifice—a turbeh with a little cupola. It is said to belong to the Hadji Baïram Mosque, and we are told that the building was raised to the memory of a Mussulman saint who was killed on the spot; then, fact lapsing into legend, it is declared that an enormous block of marble lying at our feet reached its present position by being thrown from the opposite hill against the castle by hand!

We cannot enter the interior citadel — Djin Kalé — on the extreme summit of the hill; it is now used as a powder magazine, and is difficult of access; but there was no cause for regret, as I have since been assured on the best authority that neither ancient fragments nor inscriptions are to be found in that enclosure. The situation, however, crowning as it does on the side of the ravine an immense upheaval of gigantic oblong blocks of basaltic rock, is sublime in its stern and seemingly impregnable isolation.

Amongst the ruined masses at the foot of the wall we are shown a large marble lion, bearing a very Persian aspect. Stone or marble lions seem to have been much favoured here in former times. I am told of no less than eight of these, sculptured in marble, still existing in Angora, and of one other—the most interesting of them all, mentioned and photographed by Perrot—that until lately decorated the road-side fountain of Kalaba, in the neighbourhood of the city. 'This was doubtless,' says Mr. C——, 'one of the four Phrygian lions said to have been brought to this city.' It was taken possession of by the local authorities in 1893, and sent to the museum of Tchinli Kiosque in Stamboul.

Pursuing our road through the ruins, one can form some idea of the vast extent of the castle enclosure, which during the Middle Ages was regarded as one of the most important fortresses of Asia Minor. The fortified wall (now much broken away in parts) had been strengthened throughout its entire length by towers; but oh! the hideous defacement of these venerable remains! they have been quite recently painted a bright-red colour; in some instances the red has been varied by white and blue; one large massive tower shows pale blue half-way up, the upper half scarlet; on the crenellated wall the forms are marked out in lines of vivid aniline blue upon whitewash, with central spots of scarlet; this utter depravity of taste can scarcely reach a lower depth. The line of fortified wall separates the citadel from the lower town. It is supposed that the last repairs executed here in the castle defences were due to Allah-ed-din, the last Seldjuk Sultan of Iconium, in the thirteenth century.

The bewildering amount of fragments of ancient sculpture and architecture to be found in this part of the city is almost incredible: of funereal and votive slabs; of shafts and capitals of columns; of pedestals and altars; mostly on the inner side of the encircling wall. Every chiselled stone seems to bear some ancient inscription, as you approach the old gate, now called Parmak Kapou; but before reaching it we turn aside into a small Byzantine church — not very remarkable; it also possesses a 'yan tash' (burning stone) let into the outer wall, similar to that in the Armenian monastery.

We pass on. Still more inscriptions and bits of sculpture inserted in the rough walls. On the right hand a large slab shows a cross in low relief; it forms a part of a great corner-tower, the base of which is composed of large marble slabs, the upper portion of brick and stone; the angle, enriched by a beautiful fragment of frieze-work, brings into view an extent of wall of which the destination and purpose is not apparent. Several mutilated statues in high relief are inserted lengthways near the base; one square block seems to represent angels or cupids, the whole mingled with inscriptions and thickly plastered with whitewash. Near to this curious wall we find the small mosque built by Allah-ed-din III., the Seldjuk Sultan to whose beneficent and enlightened rule many religious and useful constructions, elegant in style and rich in decoration, are ascribed. Angora, conquered and taken from the Seldjuk princes by Murad I., has rapidly declined from that time; all those traces of past wealth and prosperity—sculptures, Greek and Latin inscriptions, bridges, roads, edifices of all kinds—are falling year by year into more hopeless and absolute ruin. But this mosque of Allah-ed-din is an exception; it has been quite recently thoroughly repaired, and the columns and other remains of heathen temples originally used in its construction are still plainly visible.

Beside the mosque, a very small Turkish

cemetery shows several oblong slabs supporting the railings of the enclosure ; each slab bears an ancient inscription.

Perrot says of this neighbourhood : ' If the crumbling walls on either side of Parmak Kapou were to be demolished, hundreds of inscriptions would infallibly be brought to light.'

We left Angora with much regret, feeling that a longer time than our three days' stay might have been delightfully employed, and, being obliged by railway arrangements to pass the night at Eskischeïr, decided to spend one day there in order to visit some remains of the ancient Doryleum.

At a short half-hour's drive from the station hotel, we reach a broad district of low grass and bramble-covered hillocks, broken-up mounds and deep holes, in which men are busily working, taking out huge blocks of stone or marble. We had met on the road several rude carts heavily laden, and we were disposed at first greatly to admire the fine native zeal for antiquarian research, until it was explained that the country round possessed no stone-quarries, and that the stone-workers were simply seeking for material to be cut up for house-building. One long trench certainly showed, deep down, remains of a basement of wall of cut and chiselled marble, with indications of coping-stone and ornamental work; other holes revealed corners and fragments of white marble gleaming through the brown earth. Many columns and interesting fragments of antiquity have been long since carted away for the benefit of the town of Eskischeïr, which, from being a world-forgotten place, is now rapidly rising into importance as a junction railway-station, from which lines to Kutaya, Koniah, and on towards Smyrna, are already opened out in their nearer sections.

We did not see the famous meerschaum mines. They are at some distance in another direction, and are also practically difficult of access, as the precious material is reached through deep wells sunk far below the surface. The trade in meerschaum is pursued with great profit and activity. It is found embedded like the kernel of a nut in large formless lumps of seemingly gray clay.

The town of Eskischeïr, on a rising ground a short distance from the railway, has few attractions to offer. A large and rather pretentious hotel, some municipal buildings, and modern dwelling-houses in the upper quarter, exhaust the list of the best-meaning guide. The bazaars are poor and insignificant, but some pleasant woodland scenery on the lower slopes of the neighbouring hills may offer compensation to the inhabitants of the place.

HISTORY OF ANCYRA.

LEGENDARY lore attributes the foundation of Ancyra (the ancient name of Angora) to Midas, making it thus a Phrygian city; but a fact that is not disputed is the importance attached to the occupation of the place by Alexander the Great during his march across Asia Minor.

Perrot, in his great work, 'La Galatie et la Bithynie,' rejects the usual explanation of the name 'Ancyra,' and seeks its derivation from a Sanscrit word 'ankas,' a curve, as applying to the situation of the city rising above narrow and curved ravines. When Galatia became a Roman province, Ancyra, the capital, was renamed Sebaste, and the most beautiful monument in the city was the stately temple dedicated to 'The God Augustus and The Goddess Rome,' of which very important remains may still be seen. The worship paid to Augustus and to his successors lasted until Christianity — very early brought into Galatia—became established there after the cessation of the persecutions under Diocletian; it is even supposed that St. Paul preached here to the Galatians. St. Clement, who afterwards became its patron saint, suffered martyrdom in the city. On the spread of Christianity, Ancyra became an Apostolic see.

During the fourth century Ancyra was esteemed one of the most learned and cultivated cities of Asia Minor. An old author even compares it to Athens, and speaks of the refinement and intelligence to be found amongst the inhabitants, and praises the beauty of the climate of the neighbouring hills, rich in beautiful trees, in sparkling waters, in abundant fruits, in luxuriant vegetation. It is to this day regarded as a health resort.

Ancyra, protected by its fortress, which during the Middle Ages passed for one of the most important in Asia Minor, seems to have retained its prosperity until the beginning of the seventh century, when it was taken by the Persians in A.D. 616; reconquered by Heraclius, and, about two centuries later, was again besieged and pillaged by Haroun-al-Rashid ; but, owing to the importance of the fortifications, and to the great stream of commerce passing through this central point towards the interior of Asia, it quickly recovered somewhat from its disasters. A durable peace, however, and some shadow of its ancient prosperity returned only with the beneficent rule of the Seldjuk dynasty, dating from the end of the eleventh century.

These Seldjuk princes, who endowed their principal city, Iconium (now Koniah), with colleges, mosques, and palaces, founded also at Ancyra many important buildings, of which rich fragments still remain. The finest of these are attributed to Allah-ed-din III. (1220-1237).

In the early part of the fourteenth century Ancyra was taken from the Seldjuks by Murad I., and since that time all memories of past splendour —sculptures, Greek and Latin inscriptions, bridges, roads, public edifices—have been gradually falling into decay and disappearing.

It is difficult, without seeing them, to imagine the immense number of fragments of architecture, of votive and funereal monuments, of shafts and capitals of columns, pedestals and altars, to be remarked within the enclosure of the city wall, and in the still higher part, in the neighbourhood of the gate called Parmak Kapou. 'There is a stretch of wall that contains a long band formed of pedestals, altars, and heads of Medusa ; this curious wall is supported on masses of rough brickwork, and beneath, on marble blocks, may be read two inscriptions to the effect that the work of reconstruction took place under the Byzantine Emperor Michael' (Perrot). Local tradition affirms that the last repair of the fortifications was executed by order of the Seldjuk Sultan Allah-ed-din.

SUMMER DAYS IN CHALCEDON, 1865.

JORGHI, the Greek servant, calls this place Halkithòn. The Turks have named it Kadikeuy, or the village of the Kadi, and I know it as the best and most enjoyable of all the pleasant villages that line the sparkling shores of the Bosphorus.

During the absence of my husband in England I am spending a brief summer holiday here with kind friends, whose charming house stands in a corner of the vineyard which formerly covered the whole of the little promontory called Moda Bournou. It was celebrated for its fine 'tchaoush' grapes, and, until within a few years, was innocent of modern brick and mortar; but the tide of public favour has begun to set this way, and houses are rapidly springing up in all directions. You might imagine it a suburb of some small provincial town in France, were it not for a large green tent in the neighbouring field, which quickly

undeceives you. This is inhabited by a family
of Montenegrins. They sleep in their tent, but
pass the greater part of the day under a spreading
tree in front of our house. The kitchen-range is
set up amongst the roots of a fine mastic-tree.
The owner of the tent, who struts about gorgeous
in gold-braided jackets and a belt full of ornamental weapons, and who commands his servant
with the air of an emperor, is called by the neighbours Prince of Montenegro, as he lays claim to
be connected by marriage with the ruler of his
small country. Nevertheless, the princess, his
wife . . . takes in washing ! at so many piastres
the dozen, and she certainly acquits herself to our
satisfaction, quite as if she had been accustomed
to it all her life. This green tent under the trees,
with its half-wild occupants, recalls the Eastern
element to the picture.

My friend's house, built nearly on the verge of
the cliff, is a delightful dwelling, such as London
auctioneers would describe as 'a desirable villa
residence.' On the ground-floor a cool marble
hall leads through a rustic porch, heavy with
clematis and passion-flower, into a bright garden
all sparkling with sunshine and gay blossoms.

Of this part of the small domain I must say, as the greatest praise, that it is simply a garden, not a park, or pleasure-grounds, or parterres, or anything too grand or too extensive for the care of the two gentlemen who, aided by a Croat, make its cultivation the healthy employment of their spare moments; a garden with just the slightest suggestion of the cottage about it, to give it a thoroughly comfortable look; a garden where the flowers are intended to be plucked (discreetly), where, through the waving masses of the rose-covered trellised walk, you may discover healthy green-peas and robust cabbages not ashamed to be seen in their proper place; a garden where the geraniums have not yet all become pelargoniums, and where the delicate old-fashioned scarlet fuchsia dares still to show itself beside its washed-out, sickly-looking modern sister; a border of homely, fragrant lavender blossoms modestly in one corner, and some sweet-briar bushes, delicate and scarce, are tended with peculiar care. Mixed with all these friends of childhood are others that speak of a foreign clime. Long pendant leaves of the sugar-cane are waving near the orange and lemon trees, whose bright golden fruit sets off the rich tints of a wild pomegranate; the castor-oil plant spreads abroad its large, finely-cut leaves; the snowy cotton is bursting from the pod; and the heavy yellow clusters of the Indian wheat gleam here and there beyond the 'tchaoush' vines and the waving, feathery mimosa-trees.

There is a slight paling behind a row of raspberry-bushes that marks the limit of the enclosure; beyond it, and scarcely divided to the eye, the vineyard, the avenues of trees, the azure sea, and the distant shadowy mountains. But of this tempting landscape a better view will be obtained from the terrace.

On the upper story of the house, crossing a drawing-room, from which you get a dreamy vision of Stamboul in the distance glowing through a mist of violet and gold, you reach this terrace, without which no house in the East is complete. It has been lately trellised over for the support of various delicate climbing plants, but these we do not even see. It is the view beyond which at once arrests the eye.

To the left hand, on the summit of the cliff overhanging the little bay, the college, with its warm colouring of a pinkish-gold tint, stands out in exquisite relief against the green foliage and dark purple masses of Kaïsch Dagh. This cliff falls abruptly down from the college to the bay, which is bounded on one side by a wooded headland; on the other by fine terebinth and mastic trees, with an occasional olive for variety. From the foot of Kaïsch Dagh, on the opposite shore of the bay, the land, dotted with villas and 'tchiftliks,' and rich in clumps of trees, green shady lanes, and pleasant fields, runs out into the blue Marmora, until it narrows to a point marked by a magnificent group of plane-trees; but there, as if unwilling yet to leave the clear mirror which is reflecting all its beauties, it shoots out again, a long tongue of land covered with stately cypresses. A white old-fashioned lighthouse stands on the extreme point, and harmonizes well with the surrounding scenery. This promontory is called by the Greeks Fanaraki; by the Turks, Fanar Bagtché (Garden of the Lighthouse). The ancient name was Hereïon.

In the foreground of the picture, there, at our very feet, is the rustic walk, bordered by the terebinth and mastic trees overhanging the water,

FANARAKI.

where the *élite* among the Kadikiotes stroll up and down to display their dresses, or sit on low stools to sip the coffee supplied from a small coffee-shop at the entrance of the walk.

This is the most favoured spot of all. Here Riza Pasha, the fallen Minister of Abdul Medjid, may often be seen sitting on one of the square stools enjoying the refreshing breezes of the bay, while he smokes his narghilé. He comes quite simply now, with perhaps a single attendant; for, though still wealthy, he is a broken man, and greatly aged since the days of his full-blown prosperity.

Just beneath this favourite lounge is the new stone scala, where all our little boats—the *Polly*, the *Lucy*, the *Janie*, the *Ada*, and others—are moored, and lie in safety under the care of the cafedji. Here, as the glowing ardour of the day begins to abate, the energetic British members of the little colony collect, and rowing matches come off under the wondering eyes of the listless Levantines, to whom unnecessary exertion is a subject of intense astonishment.

Let us look up to the high ground, behind the College, there; all is bustle and activity in and about the short row of houses which have clustered together for the benefit of fresh air, sea-bathing and quiet (?). There is a German hotel and a French hotel, both full of visitors, who group themselves about the doors as the shadows of evening begin to fall, and their voices reach us at intervals across the grassy slope; there, also, as surely as the gray tints creep upwards upon the bright-coloured College wall, four merry little black ponies, with four merry little riders, trot briskly upwards, and stop at the door of the third house in the row. Then dinner-bells ring, and the bustling, active, outdoor life subsides for a time, to wake up once more about two hours later. If there is moonlight, you then see groups of idlers again lounging backwards and forwards; all the windows are open, and sounds of music float upwards, while we are perhaps engaged in a merry contest at bagatelle. But this is the end of our day; the earlier hours, happy as we ourselves feel them to be, deserve a few words of remembrance, although there is little excitement and less of adventure in our daily life.

The bell clangs loudly at half-past six in the morning; and after breakfast our host and T. T., who forms part of the family, start for a twenty minutes' walk to the steamer that carries them to their occupations on the European shore—for we are in Asia. Before leaving, however, the gentlemen who are devoted to their garden have found time to visit their pet plants. T. T. (not Tiny Tim, but Trusty Thomas) has seen that his seedling geraniums and oranges and lemons are thriving, and Mr. C—— reports that the heavy wealth of the Banksia roses has broken the light trellis-work of the garden walk. Then they depart, and, the masculine element being thus happily disposed of, we begin that cheerful mixture of practical and intellectual pursuits which keeps every faculty healthy and alive. One day, perhaps, there is some fruit to be picked for preserving, for a man has come round with a bargain in red currants (rather a rarity here), and the opportunity must not be lost; so, as the servants are all busy, we tuck up our sleeves, put on aprons, and set to work in a pleasant morning-room, with folding doors wide open upon the arbour of passion-flower and clematis, with the bright garden beyond, all sparkling and joyous in the sunshine.

We are a very happy little party of four ladies; in fact, we are so well satisfied with each other's society and with our various useful or ornamental occupations of painting, music, needlework and reading, that I am afraid we do not stand very high in the estimation of the rest of the colony for preferring these to the prevailing habit of strolling listlessly into each other's houses to tell Mrs. M. or N. that 'those Miss X. Y.'s have actually got new dresses *again*, though, to be sure, they are only imitation, and very flimsy; they won't wash, for certain; but how their father affords so much finery is more than one can imagine;' or to state an opinion of 'that idle Greek maid Calliope, who, instead of sweeping her rooms, has taken her parasol and gone for a stroll down Moda, in the very heat of the day, too'; or to wonder at 'Madame V——'s dirty little servant-of-all-work, Thespinoula, who objects to go to the neighbouring bakal's for a supply of candles because she is a demoiselle, and it is not fitting that an unprotected maiden should go to a public shop.' I may observe that, in general, Thespinoula flaps about the house in slippers and stockingless feet; she wears her uncombed hair hanging in a tail down her back from under a dirty rag that once was white, while her garments display an absence of superfluity at times almost distressing; yet on fête days she expands like a gaily-decked umbrella, and her head is adorned with one of the prettiest of coiffures, the light handkerchief, with its border of 'biblibi,' forming a coronal of bright-coloured silk flowers.

These Greek servants are an independent race, quick-witted in general, and capable of becoming good domestics, but they have their peculiarities. I knew a few years ago an honest and faithful servant whose wits might be said to be nowhere; his sayings and doings became proverbial, and he answered to the name of Nicodemus. 'Oh, what have you done?' exclaimed my friend Madame F—— in dismay; 'you have broken my vase, my beautiful vase; it is ruined—I can never replace it.'

'Madame,' replied Nicodemus calmly, 'do not distress yourself; the harm is not so great, for I have only broken one half of it; the other half is all right.'

Mr. F—— directed that the remainder of a bottle of rare wine should be put aside, and was astonished to see a full bottle appear at table the next day. 'I did as you wished, sir,' observed Nicodemus; 'there was some other wine in that bottle already, but that does not signify, as I took care to pour the good wine quite on the top.'

But I have wandered from our morning-room, with its green venetian blinds and its peeps of sea and mountain, garden and vineyard. Our kind hostess, who delights in procuring as much enjoyment as possible, is constantly planning the most delightful schemes for possible and impossible excursions, such as a picnic to Kaïsch Dagh, for which we must have horses; three or four days of tent life in the beautiful forest of Alem Dagh; a row across the bay to take our tea on the cypress-covered promontory of Fanaraki; and, lastly, a little cruise in a small steam yacht round the Gulf of Nicomedia; they are charming plans and ideas, and, if not realized, very pleasant indeed to think about. But at present we must listen to the reading, for F——, a very amiable member of our little coterie, greatly increases our enjoyment, and helps our light labours by her readiness to read aloud anything we may wish to hear for an unlimited length of time—a rare merit.

Thus our mornings glide away. About noon we dine; then, if the day be very warm, we retire to take a siesta in our rooms, from which we are aroused by the afternoon coffee; after this it is time to dress again, for at five o'clock a firm, decided, possessive knock resounds through the house, announcing the return of the gentlemen. When there is moonlight, and the plans are for a boating excursion later in the evening, a substantial meat tea is spread in the arbour under the flowering limes at the bottom of the garden. The table is decorated with flowers, the air scented with sweetbriar, Schio jasmine, orange-blossom, and all the various perfumes of the daintily kept parterres; and, just beyond the paling, a wild pomegranate lights up the scene with its scarlet clusters.

Sometimes our repast is made at Fanaraki, the long point of land covered with those wonderful old cypresses, where formerly stood a summer palace of the Greek emperors, built by Justinian on the site of the temple of Juno, and where also were erected two churches, baths, and other public buildings,; in the midst of the grove of ancient weird-looking trees, and on the adjoining tract of land, some slight remains of the former buildings may be traced in a ruined cistern, and crumbling heaps of ancient brickwork. Along the shore eastwards, considerable ruins of masonry, with fragments of marble columns, slabs and great quantities of mosaic tesseræ, to be gathered from amongst the pebbles, still further testify to the importance of the buildings that must formerly have adorned this spot.

The cypresses of Fanaraki are the most gaunt and strange-looking specimens of the kind that can be seen. They are without doubt of great age, as almost every tree has another tree of a different kind—terebinth, wild pear, fig—growing from the very centre of its branches, and these, also, show signs of long duration.

I am sitting in the vineyard with Lulu, my little Macedonian dog, at my feet; the scene is a curious mixture of nature and civilization, in which nature has the decided advantage. In front I see the scattered dwellings of the European colony of Moda Bournon; from one or two of these the strains of the educational piano, in

MODA BOURNOU.

To face p. 92.

various stages of progress, come floating over the tops of the vines, and I catch now a few bars from Gounod's 'Faust'; now some painfully uneven scales; a feeble voice is asking anxiously: 'What are the wild waves saying?' a distant water-wheel emits agonizing groans; a man is crying tomatoes in the lane beyond.

The great trunk of the stone pine which hides from me the last of the houses forms a rustic frame-work between this picture of miniature town-life and another as dissimilar as can well be imagined. Close by, on the other side of the rough bark, a field of Indian corn, with its beautiful plumes of blossom and long pendant leaves, rustles gently in the breeze, which murmurs through the branches of the pine, and breathes softly on the green tops of the fruit-trees, making Nature's own sweet melodies full of soothing harmony and rest. The ground slopes downward, and through the grove of trees one beautiful opening is filled by the deep blue waters of the Gulf of Nicomedia, with its wall of solemn mountains, and, still again beyond, a visionary outline of the snow-capped summit of the Bithynian Olympus.

I turn to the left. Here the vineyard has been sadly neglected; the proprietor, seized with a mania for building, has allowed the precious vines, that yielded the delicious 'tchaousch' grape, to remain for the most part uncared for; they are stunted and barren; but the rich earth is not to be cheated of its ornaments, and the field is bright with lilac masses of the wild hollyhock amongst feathery plumes of grass in flower. A Croat is watching his flock of silky-haired goats, white and brown, and mouse-coloured, and golden-hued; they browse round about, finding rare feeding on the green shoots of the neglected vines.

A vineyard in Turkey does not mean simply a tract of land devoted to the cultivation of the vine; it is a pleasure-ground, where the vine certainly holds the principal place, but which is a garden and orchard at the same time, full of many kinds of fruit-trees and flowering shrubs. Some of the vineyards overhanging the Bosphorus are celebrated for their beautiful roses, and for the admirable style of their adornment, with kiosks and fountains, shrubberies and winding paths kept in perfect order.

This point of Moda Bournon, known as

Tubini's vineyard, has no pretensions to landscape gardening; but it has one remarkable feature of its own: the whole of the little promontory, as well as a considerable inland tract of land, was evidently—in some bygone age—the site of an ancient cemetery; the whole of the earth is mixed with—indeed, almost composed of—broken bits of funereal amphoræ; you have but to stoop to pick up more fragments of such pottery than you can carry. They are mostly of a coarse quality, although we frequently find remnants of the smaller black or coloured and highly-glazed vases which the ancients placed inside the large funereal urns. In one part of the cliff, where the earth had fallen away, hundreds of small earthenware lamps were found, placed in rows, as if in some storehouse of a pottery.

Strolling along the upper pathway, that gives the impression of having been an avenue of the better class of tombs, we found the broken parts of two larger lamps and some pieces of finely painted vases, which, for colouring and delicacy of design, remind one of the precious relics of Etruscan art; everywhere lie strewn about large fragments of the coarse square bricks that covered some of the graves, many of them slightly coloured.

While we were groping at the foot of a fig-tree, the Croat guardian of the vineyard came near to inspect our proceedings, imagining, perhaps, that we were interested in the tomatoes, whose bright scarlet balls were peeping out all around from under their green leaves; but I quickly explained that our object was 'stones,' very, very old—quite of the ancient time. He seemed much struck with the novelty of the idea; he settled his fez, and said :

' Mashallah! when we were digging up this land we found a great many large pieces, and one big jar.'

'Well, and what did you do with it ?'

'Oh! it was of no use; it had a hole, so we broke it up and strewed the little bits all about.'

I am not sufficiently learned in these matters to pretend to fix any date to these remains. I can only remark that they resemble precisely in form and texture those which I brought away from the site of ancient Pella, in Macedonia, and that M——, my great ally in these groping expeditions, declares them to be exactly similar to those which are quite commonly found in the Troad.

On the opposite side of the bay, under a group of magnificent plane-trees, is a holy spring, called by the Greeks St. John's Well. The well itself presents no remarkable feature, except that it has been lately spoiled by the erection of an ugly whitewashed chapel; but a little higher up, on the border of the road, you find a large mass of ancient brick and stone work; an old tree of great size, growing from out the ruins, shows that it must have lain there for a considerable period. A little further along the winding, shady lane which is the highroad towards Bagdad, you come upon the remains of an ancient amphitheatre, or, perhaps, of a vast cistern.

Such ruins are scattered all over the country. Often in long rides about Constantinople, in the wildest and most sequestered nooks, remains of fountains and water-conduits are found, where for miles along those swelling uplands there is now no trace of present human care and forethought. Scarce a tree throws its shade on those hills which now blush with the soft pink of the flowering cistus, now glow with the rich tints of broom, heath and lavender. The sweet scent of wild thyme rises with each touch of our horses' feet; and mingling with the hum of the summer insect, the tinkle of some distant goat's bell alone reminds us that we are not utterly solitary in this grand and beautiful desolation. But formerly the scene must have been widely different, when the fountains and the water-pipes formed part of that complete system of irrigation by means of which this now barren wilderness bloomed like a garden in the days of Byzantine splendour.

In the immediate neighbourhood of the city, and over the slopes behind the villages of the Bosphorus, the ground has been of late years much more cultivated, chiefly in strawberries; but these are said to be almost entirely the result of French enterprise and industry.

UNDER THE OAKS AT MERDIVENKEUY.

To spend a quiet day under the spreading oaks of Merdivenkeuy, a village three or four miles distant from Moda Bournon, was a project of long standing. We accomplished it yesterday.

Our kind hostess, who is great in the commissariat department on these occasions, had caused sundry preparations to be made, in the form of chicken-pie, rhubarb-tart, roast veal, etc. The china and glass had been packed, neither the salt nor the teapot omitted, and everything was in readiness in good time for the arrival of the equipage.

For greater convenience, and a little also for the sake of the *couleur locale*, an araba had been ordered—not a painted pumpkin, or an ornamented pill-box, such as are commonly used, the proper name of which is ' talika,' but the real genuine article, a bullock-cart. These conveyances are mostly preferred for country parties, where the roads are too rough for the strength of horses, or the frail timbers of the talika; they are gaily decked and ornamented. The body of our araba was much enlivened by paint and gilding; the wheels, and the poles to sustain the awning, bright blue and red; the awning itself of a rich carmine-coloured woollen stuff, of native manufacture, with a handsome gold fringe drooping in front. Our two white oxen also were magnificent, with their broad frontlets covered with bits of looking-glass inserted in a thick embroidery of beads and spangles, the whole trimmed round with tufts of scarlet wool. Fixed to the yoke in front, and curving gracefully backwards, two long slender red poles supported strings of scarlet tassels, which sway gracefully with every movement. You get into the machine by a movable wooden ladder of six steps, and as the vehicle is not furnished with seats, the natives place mattresses on the planks and crouch upon them; in our case cushions had been charitably provided, and we were soon comfortably en route—four ladies and a little child within the araba, two Armenian servants perched somewhere about the shafts. Mr. E——, a young English clergyman, accompanied us on horseback.

Two serious, respectable-looking Turks guided our little team, one directing their heads by admonitory pulls of their long horns, the other stimulating their solemn progress by suggestive pokes from the long wand he carried.

The araba having no springs, we were, of course, considerably shaken over the rough stones of the village street; but we soon turned aside on to a somewhat smoother road, and crossing a corner of the large meadow, came in sight of a house to which is attached a tale of local manners and customs. It is a bright, handsome, well-ordered residence, in the midst of gardens and greenhouses, fountains and orangeries, and adorned within, they say, with paintings of some value brought from Italy. Here flourishes a certain Don Andrea, now a high dignitary of the Latin Church of Kadikeuy, a wealthy and important personage, who, about four years ago, was known as Andrea Kalimaki, a modest Greek tutor in the village; and on the site of the trim modern mansion stood a pretty little rose-coloured cottage in a rambling, neglected vineyard; it belonged to a Turkish family, too poor to cultivate their land properly, so they offered it for sale; and Kalimaki, who had put by some savings, purchased the property for a small sum. There was, however, a condition attached to the sale: the Turks, who had held this land from father to son for many generations, had a family tradition that an immense treasure in jewels and money had been in ancient times buried away somewhere on the land at a great depth; they did not, perhaps, put implicit faith in their tradition; at any rate, they were too poor and too inert to undertake the necessary researches; so they sold their property with the understanding that if the purchaser found anything of value within it, the amount should be equally divided between them.

Andrea took possession of his modest cottage, and nothing particular transpired, until it was remarked by the original proprietors that the cottage was expanding into a mansion; that the tangled vineyard was blossoming into pleasure-gardens; and that the humble tutor had evidently become a wealthy man. They claimed their half of the recovered treasure—to which rumour ascribed a fabulous amount—but the voice of the earthen pipkin is small when raised against the golden vase. Don Andrea turned a deaf ear for a time, until the matter was referred to Rome, whither he was suddenly summoned. On his return everyone seemed satisfied; and Don Andrea is now a cheery, hearty old gentleman, enjoying his rare good fortune in peace.

After passing the whole length of what we still call the cricket-field, our araba brought us out upon the plain, at the foot of Kaïsch Dagh, which rose majestically in front, with its beautiful outline and heather-tinted sides. To the left of the road a deep ravine marked the course of an insignificant streamlet, beyond which the land was rich with melon-fields and maize, both in blossom, the bright yellow flowers of the melon forming a beautiful contrast to the graceful feathery violet bloom that drooped from the tall stalks of the Indian corn. Beyond the melon beds, the threshing-floors were in full activity, the oxen literally, as in Scripture phrase, 'treading out the corn'— one man urging them with the goad, while another sat on the threshing-board to increase its weight.

Our adventures in the short transit to Merdivenkeuy were of the mildest description, being merely an occasional violent plunge of one wheel into a mud-hole, eliciting a quickly stifled wail from the little boy, and four screams, with an immediate proposal on our part to alight and walk ; but the old Turk, who seemed to understand perfectly what he was about, would raise his finger with a warning 'soos' (silence), and we contented ourselves with clinging to the hoops of the awning, or preparing to fall as softly as possible into each other's laps.

Before reaching the village, we passed a frail-looking wooden bridge, which had been thrown over the crumbling remains of one which must formerly have been of greater importance ; the broken arch is of heavy masonry, and near it are traces of ancient brickwork. A magnificent plane-tree overshadowed the spot.

The place at which our araba halted, at the entrance of the little hamlet, was charming. At first one could imagine it a somewhat neglected village green in England : spreading oaks of unusual size and beauty, intermingled here and there with elm and plane trees, surrounded a grassy glade, dotted over with snowy geese and an occasional cow or donkey; the barn of the tchiflik, or farm, looked homely enough, rising above the smaller trees, but a second glance shows that we are in a land many of whose customs have scarcely varied for centuries; all over the gentle slope of the hills the toiling oxen of the threshing-floors, and the primitive method of sifting the wheat, looked as if winnowing-machines and the endless string of modern farming improvements existed not.

While the servants are preparing our early dinner at the foot of a stately oak, we wander about, to look at the groups of Turkish women who are crouched on carpets round their mid-day meal. The summer life of these women is very much of a picnic existence; they frequently pack up their carpets, their cushions, and their children, and are conveyed to some green shade, or near some sparkling fountain, where they make themselves perfectly at home for the day. If a baby is of the party, they begin their temporary installation by knotting a shawl at the four corners, and, swinging it between two trees, the little hammock bed is, in two minutes, just the same as it would be in the home, where large rings are fixed into the woodwork of the rooms for this purpose.

There were some pretty girls among the groups of women sitting on the green at Merdivenkeuy; two of them, in crimson satin feradjis, especially attracted us. They had lowered their yashmaks for convenience of eating, and we could see their small delicate features, and calculate the amount of paint which was in favour with each one. A striking-looking Abyssinian slave, with an apology for a yashmak floating over her head and shoulders, warmed up the dishes over a little fire of dry sticks. Another party of four ladies, more rigid in their ideas of propriety, got into their carriage whenever they wished for a perfectly unveiled face and a quiet smoke They strolled near us while we dined, and seemed greatly to admire our 'spread,' but they were perfectly ladylike and unobtrusive.

Not so an ancient dame in tatters of a Greek cut and fashion: she hobbled towards us as soon as we were seated, with her knitting in one hand and a long wand in the other, and squatting down at the foot of a neighbouring tree, fell hard to work, but staring at us unremittingly all the while; she only interrupted her knitting to make occasional onslaughts on the wild dogs, who, doubtless, judg-

AT MERDIVENKEUY.

To face p. 106.

ing that she had intentions of poaching on their rights to the remnants of the feast, were disposed to treat her as an open enemy; she beat them off, however, and immediately subsided on to her heels, knitting and staring as before. As soon as we had finished, the old hag suggested that it would be fitting that she also should dine; her wish was gratified, and we passed on, ignoring the subsequent hint of 'backshish.'

The parties of Turkish women whom we had found on the ground on our arrival left early and drove off to end the day at Fanaraki, where there is a fashionable native promenade on Fridays; but later in the afternoon two more talikas drove up and deposited their freights, consisting of three very young women and a minute baby. They were accompanied by two men, which is so unusual a proceeding, and one so contrary to Mussulman ideas of propriety, that one could but conclude that they were persons of a very inferior station. They were very quiet and well-behaved, however, and the baby was a curiosity; swathed in a small shawl, with its tiny feet and hands projecting, it looked like a good-sized chrysalis, as one of the young men—the father, probably—

danced and caressed the little bundle. He appeared very proud of it, and brought it to us to be admired. The man was dressed as a touloumbadji, or fireman, with immensely baggy trousers and tight legs, and as for some reason he had turned his peaked hood over his head, the whole outline was most comical. The mother, we found, was the youngest-looking of the group—a pretty little pale thing about fourteen years old. We left her nursing the little one as we turned to leave, and looking round soon afterwards, saw her cherry-coloured satin cloak flying gaily in the wind on the crest of the hill, while she was being whirled round with one of her companions on the threshing-board.

We left the peaceful shades of Merdivenkeuy very reluctantly, and climbing once more into our ornate but springless araba, progressed only too quickly homewards, for every moment deepened the long shadows on the breezy common that led towards Kadikeuy. Stamboul, in the soft distance, was putting on its opal-tinted veil, while in the clear evening sky above us one feathery cloud, touched here and there with gold, had taken the form of an angel with outspread wings, holding towards the distant city a shadowy crown or garland, seeming an emblem of rest and peace.

An emblem of rest and peace? Alas! since those few words were written the very darkness of the grave has shrouded that doomed city. The fearful sickness—cholera—brought in the first instance by the scared Egyptians flying in wild terror from the scourge at Alexandria, has fallen on Constantinople with a violence which the utmost efforts of the Government have been unable to avert. To arrest the spread of the epidemic by quarantine regulations would appear to be impossible. The awe-stricken people fled in blind confusion: some to die by hundreds on the crowded boats which carried their reeking freight towards distant coasts, where already the strange, mysterious malady, spreading with giant strides, grimly awaited the few survivors; others, to strew the high-roads into the interior with the corpses of the hapless creatures who sank and died where they fell, happy if some scanty tree or barren rock shielded their last agonies from the piercing rays of the sickening sun.

Now, as I write, the fatal visitation has been mercifully permitted to diminish its ravages; how many have been swept away by it—in Stamboul especially—will never be ascertained, as the official returns are supposed to give less than one-third of the real number of deaths. It is known that in one day, of which the published number was little over 300, 700 victims to cholera were carried for interment through the Adrianople Gate—one only of the numerous gates that lead from the city to the neighbouring cemetery. On another day sixty imâms were borne to their last resting-place by the same road; and during the worst period of the sickness 2,000 a day is supposed to be within the number of deaths in Stamboul and the villages of the Bosphorus; but the darkest secrets of this time of terror will never be revealed on earth. Numbers, they say, found a hasty, even a living, grave in the silent waters of the Sea of Marmora, thrown over on the first sign of illness from fishing-boats and from the great bazaar caïques, which ply between St. Stefano and the Capital. I was told by an inhabitant of the former place that of one boat-load of twenty-seven persons which left there, six or seven only reached the landing-place ; and, allowing largely for the exaggerations of fear, I must believe, from what I know of the degree of abject terror which had seized the native population, with their general carelessness of human life, that there was much truth in these reports.

Our village of Kadikeuy, that escaped a former visitation of cholera, has been on this occasion heavily afflicted, twenty a day being carried off from the small population during the worst period. Sometimes in the night-time unwonted footsteps and the hushed voices of men passed the house in the direction of the landing-place. We did not inquire why the stillness of the dark hours was thus broken, but we knew afterwards that the sick and the dead were being carried to the boats which conveyed the former to the hospital, the latter— we knew not whither.

The disease declared itself at first in the arsenal, and spread rapidly to the surrounding localities of Haskeuy and Kassim Pasha, where it carried off great numbers of the low Jewish population; to bad drainage and the poor way of living of the unhappy Jews was mainly due the spread of infection, but they increased the danger by eating the unwholesome vegetables which had been thrown away into the Golden Horn by order of the authorities.

The English employed in the arsenal workshops, many of whom live at Haskeuy, remained stoutly at their posts when all the native workmen had fled in terror; at first they suffered slightly, but when the Government found it necessary to relieve the overcrowded cemeteries of Stamboul by sending the bodies to their uncoffined graves on the hill of the Ocmeïdan, above the village, then the English sickened and died. Some—too many, I fear—paid in that awful moment the penalty of intemperance, but there were good and gentle women among them who remained in the infected neighbourhood rather than increase the panic by their flight. One, the wife of a principal engineer, said to a friend of ours: 'My husband wishes me to leave Haskeuy, and I should like to go; but I think it would discourage the people, so I prefer to remain here.' She remained; the next day she sickened, and on the following afternoon it was Mr. K——'s sad duty to read the burial service over her in the English cemetery of Ferikeuy.

The unhappy Turks, in the height of the

calamity, caused processions of imâms to traverse the streets of the city and of the suburbs at night, barefoot, crying to the Almighty to have pity on the plague-stricken people; they even prayed some Christian communities to join them in these litanies. I do not know whether the request was complied with. I cannot think with those who ridicule this movement, and ask what has become of the stoicism of Moslem 'Khismet.' I sympathize rather with the gentleman who raised his hat as the procession passed, and was pleased to see the satisfaction which this slight mark of good feeling appeared to afford them. Christian and Moslem, children of one Heavenly Father, suffering under one common calamity, should we not together 'cry unto the Lord in our trouble'?

Our happy summer days are clouded with tears. Our little household—thank God for it!—has passed unharmed through this fearful time of sickness; and this safety I attribute greatly—under Providence—to the healthy, cheerful, rational tone of our friend's home. While the public offices were closed, the Exchange shut up, and the deserted streets of Galata testified to the extent of the panic, our English gentlemen have continued to go bravely to their daily avocations, in spite of the harrowing sights and tales of woe which met them there; they did not speak of them on their return, but we surmised much of the truth; and, without giving way to overpowering fear, we never for one moment altogether forgot the solemn dispensation which overshadowed us, although our daily course of employment remained unchanged.

The cloud that has fallen over us, the sadness of all around, has dimmed the brightness of the glorious landscape; our pleasant plans and projects have faded away, and yet!—perhaps—one day we may begin to speak of them again. Yesterday they said that the snow-white gulls have returned; they were seen in myriads, circling in their flight back to the shores of the Bosphorus, and people now remember that during the late time of sickness all birds had been unaccountably absent; that the storks had taken flight a month before their usual time, as if the mysterious taint in the atmosphere—unfelt by man's coarser senses—were perceptible to the delicate instincts of animal life; but the snowy birds have come once more, and the soft summer of the later season may yet bring to those who have been mercifully spared many a calm and happy day in bright Chalcedon.

GENERAL VIEW OF BROUSSA, 1866.

A BRIGHT morning in May; through the open windows of the little Hôtel Loschi the soft breeze reaches us direct from the mountains on the opposite side of the richly-cultivated plain, stirring with a gentle murmur the topmost branches of the trees that grow far beneath the high rocky terrace on which the hotel stands. There is a sweet trilling of birds' voices; no other sound to break the peaceful calm, until from the leafy depth arises a soft, low, solemn chant; it rises and falls, and is answered at intervals by a sort of chorus. We look beneath, at the point where a lofty poplar and a wide-spreading Oriental plane join their deep shadows to that of a group of walnut-trees on the opposite side of the winding road, where a narrow, irregular lane leads off in the direction of Mondania and the shore of the gulf. This point is a rural trysting-

OLD ROMAN BRIDGE, BROUSSA.

To face p. 116.

place—of meeting and of parting—where friends wait to welcome the coming guest, and where travellers leaving Broussa bid farewell to those who have accompanied them thus far on their road.

Such trysting spots, called in Turkish 'aïrylik mahalessi' (the place of parting), are frequently met with in the East, on the outskirts of towns. Sometimes it consists of a small building, looking like an empty 'turbeh;' I have seen such a one outside Canea in Crete; sometimes it is a wayside fountain, as near Scutari, where it is called 'aïrylik tcheshmessi;' sometimes, as here at Broussa, only an ancient, spreading, shade-giving tree at a point where two roads meet.

The low, sad chant that has drawn us to the window rises from a party of well-dressed people on foot, slowly winding their way towards the walnut shade; there are led horses, evidently prepared for a journey, new saddles and padded cushions strapped on, the harness and everything connected with it also new.

Arrived at the trysting-place, the party of friends stops and forms a circle round an aged man, who for awhile takes up the sad, wailing dirge; the friends reply by a faint chorus; some cheer feebly, and when all sinks into silence, they press forward to kiss the old man's hand; some take him in their arms and embrace him very tenderly, then, turning away, press their hands across their eyes. It was a very solemn and touching leave-taking, and the venerable patriarch, helped up upon his newly-saddled horse, and followed by only one or two friends or attendants, passed slowly away into the leafy shadow of the wood, and was lost to sight.

We ask the meaning of this sad ceremony. The aged traveller is a Jewish hadji going to Jerusalem to end his days, and to be laid to rest in that sacred earth. He has made much money in the course of his long career, and now, feeling that life is drawing to its close, leaves all his substance to his son, who will send him for the remainder of his life a sum barely sufficient for the simplest necessaries of existence; he goes far from family and friends, alone, solitary, to die in the sacred land of his forefathers.

A few days later other hadjis create a sensation in the place; it is of joy this time, not of sorrow, and forms a striking contrast to the sad little scene so lately witnessed. During breakfast a sound of firing rises from the wooded glade, and at the same time an unusual clatter on the stony road before the house draws us once more to the window. A brilliant procession of mounted zeïbeks is passing along in a shambling, irregular manner. Every colour of the rainbow flashes from their gay dresses and from their glittering belt of weapons ; others are stationed at the trysting-place and along the road, firing salutes ; there is great excitement ; the inhabitants collect in groups, most of them resting placidly on their heels — a favourite attitude of repose in this country—and the mounted zeïbeks ride forward across the little wooden bridge to meet the pilgrims returning from Mecca.

At length these hadjis emerge from the arch of foliage, three or four of them mounted on donkeys and accompanied by many friends. A rather shabby man leads the procession ; they all look dusty and travel-stained ; some of the party have brilliant Syrian haïks thrown over the head.

In the shadow of the great walnut-tree an imâm and a few persons are waiting ; the little cavalcade stops ; the imâm advances and embraces the hadjis. At that moment a veiled woman, who has patiently remained standing for a considerable time, presses forward, and hands up her child to one of the pilgrims, who, with no apparent greeting to the mother, takes the little one before him on the saddle; the whole party wind out of the wood, turning round by the great flour-mill, and so on into the town.

Returning through Broussa that same afternoon, we found crowds of people collected in the principal roadway, expecting the arrival of more pilgrims. Numbers of veiled women were seated on the edge of the pathway, and many groups had taken up their station in the road beneath. One small party was strikingly picturesque; two of the men—one old, the other in the prime of life—wore the 'cloak of honour,' made of a thick, dark stuff of camel's hair, with a rich pattern in gold, passing in broad stripes over the shoulders, woven into it. The old man, whose countenance was of the grand calm type often seen in Broussa, but more rarely met with in Constantinople, was crowned by a magnificent turban enriched with gold thread. The younger hadji, a strikingly handsome man and very dark, wore with his cloak of honour a brilliant Syrian kefyieh; he held on his knee a lovely little blue-eyed girl, her fair hair plaited with long silver threads; they were all drinking coffee and talking very cheerfully while waiting the return of another pilgrim. We met him a few minutes afterwards, escorted by rather an imposing cavalcade. First cavasses and zabtiehs on foot, then a troup of mounted zeïbeks, brilliantly dressed, and lastly a venerable old gentleman in a ponderous cloak of honour; he wore enormous spectacles. One or two aged men, who had been straining their eyes to discern the approach of their long-lost friend, press forward as he comes slowly into sight; they kiss him, pat him on the back, and seem much affected; it was indeed very touching to see the loving welcome given to one who had come back in health and safety from an undertaking from which so many never return.

We remarked afterwards that sheep had been sacrificed on the threshold of several dwellings in Broussa, in token of thanksgiving for the safe return of the master or of one of the family; the meat on these occasions is principally given to the poor.

THE KEBAB SHOP.

OUR road lay through the bazaars, which are not remarkable in any way, unless for the abundant fountains of clear water that you find at every turn. It began to rain heavily, and we were glad to seek shelter and rest in a kebab shop, not sorry to turn the time also to account in the matter of refreshment; so we boldly make our way up some exceedingly narrow ladder-like stairs on to a gallery, where we had perceived from below some straw stools — in Levantine language ' skemlé '—and, drawing them as near as possible to the wooden railing, we gain a bird's-eye view of the cook's shop and of the process of kebab-cooking in the most genuine and orthodox manner. We see the whole business from the very beginning, short of the slaughter of the poor animal who furnishes the feast. There, in the very centre of the establishment, beside a fountain of water trembling in a white marble basin, hangs the carcase which has just been operated upon for our benefit.

The master of the kebab shop wears an embroidered turban, a red scarf of many folds, and a striped apron tightly fastened round him; he presides at the shop counter, on which are some platters and covered metal bowls, with a large dish displaying a row of kebabs ready prepared for roasting; further on, an attendant is serving a customer in the street, and still further back another is seated on the counter watching a man who is washing his hands at the fountain; a zeïbek, wearing a monstrous turban and a formidable arsenal of arms in his belt, is waiting, seated beside a small round table; a lounging boy gazes idly down from the little wooden gallery.

The shop is quite open on one side to the street, and there is an uninterrupted view of the variegated crowd filling up the narrow way: a woman on horseback with a baby in one of the panniers; a man in a green cloak and large white turban; a negro in a yellow cloak, the peaked hood raised. An endless variety of forms and colours passes slowly, until the jangle of a well-known bell forces the crowd to leave a passage in the centre for a string of camels with their noiseless footfall, slow progress, and unutterably disdainful and supercilious expression ; they have come from the interior, laden, perhaps, with chrome earth, or with the valuable lumps of meerschaum from Eski Scheir. It is a long train, but they have at length passed, and now we see a sauton holding out his begging dish ; he is stripped to the waist to allow of the due display of the evidence of his sanctity ; two iron discs are woven into the skin of one arm near the shoulder ; a skewer is larded through each temple ; another through the mouth and cheek ; his hair is long, wild and matted, and he thrusts forward his canoe-shaped metal dish with a fierce, defiant gesture ; he is a repulsive object, and we gladly turn our attention to the cook's department that more immediately concerns us.

The process of cooking kebabs is by no means a simple question of broiling little pieces of mutton ; they must be quite artistically arranged. The pieces of meat must have, if possible, a tiny portion of fat to each mouthful ; they are strung, carefully graduated in size, on iron skewers, the smallest at the bottom, and the summit crowned by a large piece of the fat tail of the Karamanian sheep, so that a gentle cascade of grease—a simple method of basting—preserves the meat from scorching; eight to ten pieces of meat form a skewerful.

Our turbaned cook takes a set of prepared skewers from an attendant, lifts the door of an oven that seems to be in the shop counter, hangs them somewhere in the glowing cavity, claps down the cover, and waits. When he judges that the meat is nearly cooked, some flaps of unleavened bread are dabbed on to the hot sides till slightly browned, then whipped out, and rapidly cut into strips on a large dish; the skewers are raised, and the little bits of rich brown meat shred down on the bread, peppered, salted, sprinkled with herbs, and served quite hot; the natives add a ladleful of grease—which we decline.

BROUSSA IN 1886.

A TOURIST gazing from the heights of Pera upon the purple mountains that border the Gulf of Nicomedia, sees, above and beyond them, a range of snow-clad summits, pale in the morning light, or touched by the golden rays of sunset; he is told that at the foot of those lofty peaks lies Broussa—the cradle of the Ottoman race—as famous for the beauty of its scenery as for the healing virtues of its mineral springs; and the energetic tourist rushes thither, to 'do' the place in one clear day, arriving on Tuesday evening, and leaving at daybreak on the Thursday; but the real traveller, the artist, the lover of old-world legends, will contrive a longer sojourn at one of the many comfortable hotels that have sprung up within the last few years, and will be richly repaid for the lengthened stay amidst these scenes of sylvan beauty by a store of 'sunny memories' of leafy groves and grassy dells, of rippling brooks and wayside fountains, of cool, soft shade and rich luxuriance of glowing blossoms, the boundless vista of the broad, cultivated plain, or of the sterner features of this enchanting spot, the cloud-capped summits and dark ravines, the giant crags, the torrent rushing through a wilderness of ferns and tangled creepers.

Broussa, within an easy summer-day's journey of Constantinople, has been, until lately, little visited, owing to the difficulties of the way and the want of hotels; at the present time we find comfortable carriages, a smooth road, and hotels that increase in number with each returning season. The place possesses also attractions of an infinitely more Oriental type and character than can now be found at Constantinople. The stately Asiatic Osmanli, so rarely seen on the European shore, sits under the spreading planetrees and smokes his 'tchibouk' in immovable tranquillity, scarcely raising his eyes to notice the restless 'Frank' who darkens his sunshine for a moment by his eager progress; while his infant grandson, in a miniature turban and largely-developed shawl girdle, looks as far behind the social impetus of the nineteenth century as his venerable grandsire. Wild picturesque peasants from the interior conduct long strings of camels laden with the raw produce of those remote districts; the very plants by the wayside indicate a semi-tropical region.

Let us look down from the castle hill, the site of the ancient Prusa, founded, it is said, by Hannibal, and later the residence of the younger Pliny, pro-Consul of Bithynia under Trajan; the view from this point is beautiful beyond description. The snowy crest of Olympus is hidden from view, but behind and far away on either side, the grand summits of the lower range rise gray, or blue, or rose-coloured, according to the varying effects of passing shadows, from out a mass of the most luxuriant foliage; above, dark forests of pine and fir tree, swelling, as they descend, into rich waves of chestnut, oak and beech, with many a solemn-hued cypress steadying the heaving flow of softened green; midway down the slopes of the mountain, a tiny minaret here and there, or a cluster of picturesque, irregular buildings, mark some téké or the tomb of a saint, some shrine more or less venerated; then behind the grassy plateau of Bounar Bashi, embosomed in the hanging groves, you mark three larger tékés, one a pale-rose colour, another yellow, the third white. Further on, the shrine of Saïd Nazir clings to the roots of a gigantic cypress; beyond, and again higher up the mountain, two rocky spurs are crested by the tombs of Abdal Murad and Abdal Musa, companions of Orkhan in his conquest of the city.

To the extreme west the view is lost in a flood of golden light sweeping across the wooded heights above the baths of Tchekirghé, catching a minaret, a cypress, or the gilded crescent of a mosque in its descent, till it strikes a spark of vivid green from the tomb of Fatma Sultana, and, softening as it reaches the light haze over the park-like plain, ripples away in little silver points along the winding course of the Niloufar.

Below the castle hill spreads out the mass of the city: you look straight down into the courts of old caravanserais and schools, and imarets and mosques, and out of the confused mingling of gray and red tints rises the majestic Olou Djami, with its nineteen domes and four gigantic minarets. The houses are rather densely packed about the bazaars, but on the further side of the ravine gardens bloom and extend their foliage around the celebrated Yeshil Djami. Far off, and beyond the city, a golden gleam comes from the beautiful mosque and tomb of Emir Sultan; it contrasts strangely with a ruined monument that arrests the eye as it wanders downwards to the plain. Gray, gaunt, and solitary, it stands on a slight rise beyond the foot of the mountain; away from the life of the city, from the smiling gardens, from the waving forests, it crowns the only dreary spot in all this wealth of beauty, and seems to tell silently its tale—the mosque of the celebrated Bajazet, begun by him in his days of barbaric splendour on a scale of corresponding magnificence, incompletely finished by his son after the country had been ruined by Tamerlane, and was then ravaged by civil war. Beyond this lonely mosque the scene brightens once more; there are wide patches of mulberry gardens and vineyards, with villages and hamlets dotting the fertile plain, until it rises into the bolder forms of the mountain range (the Arganthonios), and melts into the blue distance towards Yenisheïr, and the interior of Asia Minor.

BROUSSA IN 1896.

THE general aspect of Broussa in the present year (1896) remains, with some exceptions, such as the previous slight sketch has described it ten years earlier. In that interval, however, the railway from Mondania has been opened; a wide road now leads from the city to the iron baths of Tchekirghé, giving facility for a good service of carriages, while it has destroyed an exquisitely beautiful, though almost impracticable, bowery lane. Other roads cut ruthless, if useful, straight lines through groves whose sylvan beauty could scarcely be surpassed; a new hospital shows white and glaring upon the summit of the castle hill, where formerly a rambling wooden tenement marked the site of a summer palace of Sultan Murad II., and possibly also the site of 'my apartments in Prusa,' in which Pliny wrote many of his letters to his imperial master, Trajan.

Beyond the city a large establishment—a college for the improvement and encouragement of the silk rearing—with several detached villas, now animate the wild and beautiful upland slopes and crags that overhang the deep ravine, the Gheïk Deré, the gorge beside which the rough mule-track leads upwards towards the summit of Olympus ; but on the further side of the ravine a despairingly straight and stony carriage-road harshly invades those sylvan solitudes, and one feels painfully convinced that the essentially Oriental character of the place must inevitably fade before the inexorable march of progress, pioneered and opened out by steam and rail.

SURIDJI, BROUSSA.

To face p. 132.

IN MACEDONIA.

SOME of the following notes of travel in Macedonia have already appeared in print, although so long since that few indeed will recall them. The only excuse for their repetition may be found in the slight sketches which, trivial in themselves, are historically interesting, and may probably be the only similar records existing of the birthplace of Alexander the Great and of his Macedonian capital.

The new line of railway between Salonica and Monastir leads away from the old Roman road, the Via Egnatia, and cannot approach the beautiful Lake of Ochrida, and the ancient monastery of St. Naum, where Christianity was first brought to the Bulgarians.

CAVALLA.

IN the course of the afternoon we anchored before Cavalla—that old Neapolis where St. Paul landed on his way from Troas to Philippi and Thessalonica.

The aspect of the town is very striking, standing as it does principally on a projecting mass of rock, which rises abruptly from the sea. Half-way up, a long range of white buildings, with colonnades, cupolas, and minarets, is the Turkish college, founded by Mehemet Ali of Egypt, who was a native of this place. On the summit of the peak stands the fortress, with its round and square towers; a strong wall, apparently Saracenic, surrounds the town, and a short distance in the background a fine aqueduct of Roman work, still in good preservation, connects Cavalla with the neighbouring mountains.

The whole of this range, as seen from a window

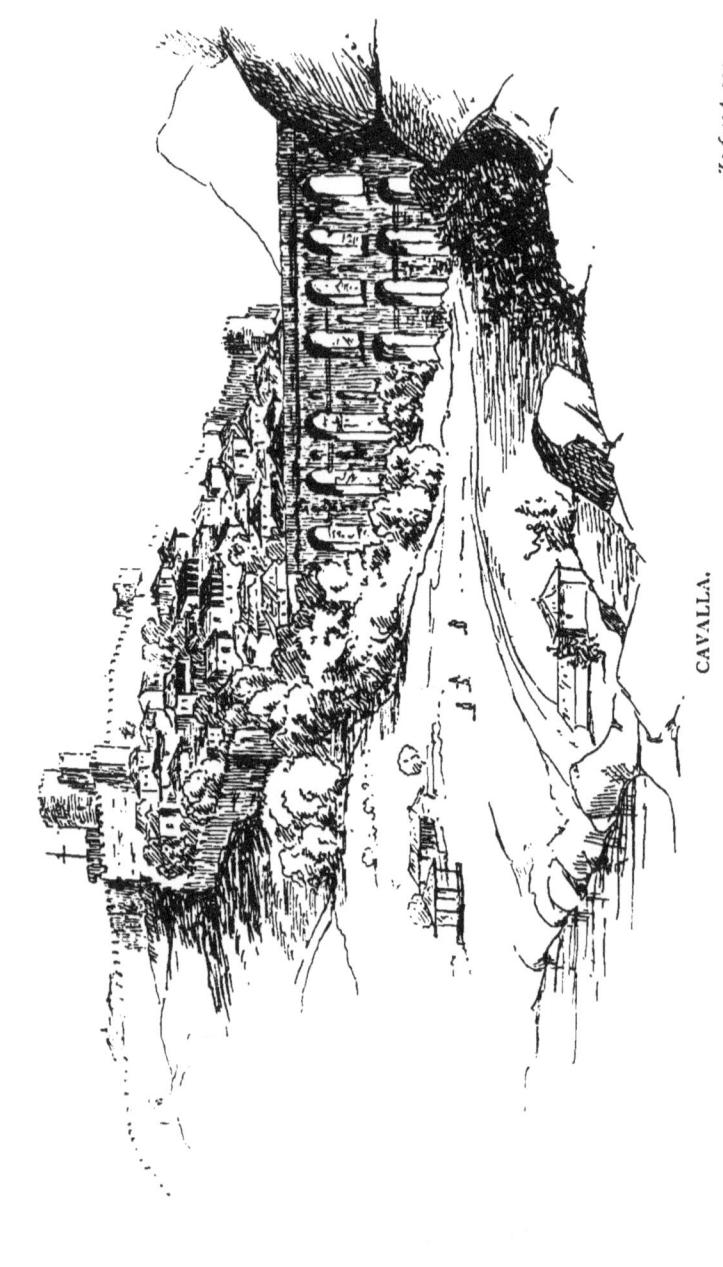

CAVALLA.

of the British Vice-Consulate, is extremely wild and barren: masses of granite, partly overgrown with low shrubs; here and there a stunted tree; two solitary watch-towers; the crumbling remains of an old Roman wall. It would seem that much in that stern landscape remains unchanged since the day when the holy Apostle of the Gentiles, staff in hand, commenced his toilsome ascent of that bleak mountain ridge, along the celebrated Roman road, the Via Egnatia, on his way to Philippi. On one part of this ridge the camp of Brutus and Cassius is supposed to have been planted before the battle of Philippi (B.C. 42), which terminated so fatally for both.

I sat long gazing on that ancient roadway. It follows the graceful curve of the bay beyond the principal mosque, with its snow-white minaret and giant plane-tree, then turns to climb the rocky height; winding round the first spur of the mountain, it disappears; more faintly and higher up, on the next projecting mass, you trace it again, irregular and broken: it plunges into a deep chasm and is lost. No; there is a silver thread melting in the vapoury haze of that distant peak, and as the eye strives to follow that celebrated mountain track, imagination flies back to the two great events with which, in those long past centuries, this road to Philippi is for ever associated.

The mosque and the minaret—are not. Along that barren roadway a glittering troop of iron-clad soldiers bear aloft the proud eagle of Rome, sparkling and flashing in the bright sunlight as they march, secure of conquest, towards their camp on the high mountain ridge; they are the stern followers of yet sterner leaders, and their struggle is for the empire of the world. A few days, and that struggle which has shaken civilization to its centre has ceased, hushed in the heaving battlefield beyond that mountain-pass. . . .

A century has nearly elapsed. Again a little band pursue their toilsome way over the rough stones, and begin to ascend the rock-bound path; they are humble men in humble garments from the opposite shores of Asia; they carry no glittering eagle, no 'weapon made with hands,' yet are they combatants, and, more, they are conquerors in the name of their Almighty Master.

The leader of this little band carries a traveller's staff to assist his weary feet as he toils higher and yet higher upwards; but the seal of the Christian martyr is on his thoughtful brow, and he bears to benighted Europe a gentle, yet unquenchable light. The cry from darkened Macedonia has mysteriously reached him on the far-off coast of Troas, and he hastens to bear to the Gentile world that heavenly flame, the all-conquering light of the Gospel.

The visionary fancy has passed away; the golden sunset throws long shadows far over the calm ripples of the blue Ægean Sea; in the faint, vapoury distance a towering, majestic form—the lofty marble crest of Athos, the Holy Mountain—gleams with the last touches of golden glory; while in the foreground Thasos, richly wooded to the water's edge, sends dark reflections far down into the liquid mirror, and loads the soft evening breeze with the aromatic perfume of its clustering pines.

PELLA.

HAVING spent several weeks at Salonica, a guest of our kind friends, Mr. and Mrs. C——, I joyfully accepted their invitation to go on with them to Monastir, to which place Mr. C—— had lately been appointed Consul.

We formed a numerous and very motley cavalcade as we left the city by the Vardar Gate. In addition to our own family, a missionary and his wife and little girl were taking advantage of the escort; there were the usual consular cavasses, servants, and miscellaneous attendants on horses and baggage, and the finishing touch of brilliancy was given by the guard of honour sent by the Pasha—wild-looking Albanians, dressed in bright colours, and bristling with weapons.

The first night was passed at Valmàthes, a small village on the great plain, sometimes called the Plain of Vardar, stretching from the gates of

Salonica to the foot of the mountain range that forms its western boundary. It is a dreary, arid, sandy level; for many miles around, the country is absolutely treeless, and the glaring rays of the sun, intensified by the glittering quality of the soil, causes the heat thrown up from the ground to be as oppressive as that so fiercely darting on us from above.

In the morning of the second day of our journey we reached the little khan of Pella, a desolate roadside caravansery, near a large fountain; it possessed, however, the blessing of a few trees, which spread their shade over a hundred feet or so of scanty grass, beside a tiny stream of running water—altogether a combination of luxuries impossible to resist; so the horses were unloaded, carpets and cushions spread in the shade beside the little rill, a picnic luncheon laid out before us, and—we rested. Fully to appreciate the happiness of shade and rest, one must know something of the Vardar plain in the month of August.

Few persons ever stop at Pella; the part of the road between Salonica and Yenidjeh is the most fatiguing, as it is also the longest stage of the journey to Monastir, and that, perhaps, is the reason why so little search seems hitherto to have been made for remains of the old Macedonian city. Most travellers, anxious to push forward towards their shelter for the night, content themselves with a glance at the old wall on the hill to the right, and a draught of the clear water of the fountain below; nothing more meets the notice of a casual observer, but it is probable that anyone having time and means to excavate and examine the ground in the little village of Neokhori, at a short distance from the fountain, which has been identified with a portion of ancient Pella, would be rewarded for his trouble. Mr. C—— rode up to Neokhori and found some subterranean sculptured columns, but was not able to examine further. Colonel Leake, in his work on 'Northern Greece,' speaks of the fountain as 'a copious source which is received into a square reservoir of masonry, and flows out of it in a stream to the marsh. This source is called by the Bulgarians "Pel." As the ancient cities of Greece often derived their names from a river or fountain, the same may have occurred in the instance of the celebrated capital of Philip and his successors, which the description of Livy, compared with the tumuli and other ancient remains, clearly shows to have stood in this situation. It would seem as if the name of Pella survived even the ruins of the city, and had reverted to the fountain to which it was originally attached.'

I went up the hill through a stubbly field to examine the remains of masonry called the ruins of the palace of Philip. It is a crumbling bit of wall of rough stones put together with mortar, and to my unlearned eye it did not bear the stamp of so great antiquity. The other remains, at the foot of the hill, have a more genuine look; the reservoir into which the waters of the source are collected, as well as the large fountain beneath (by the side of the road and opposite to the khan), are constructed of solid square blocks of stone, certainly of ancient date; they are quite out of proportion to the present insignificance of the modern halting-place.*

Coins are found in great abundance in all the lands around, as well as pottery and inscribed

---

* Rev. H. Tozea, in 'The Highlands of Turkey,' calls this 'a ruined mass of Roman masonry.'

stones. Quite recently the trenches cut on either side of the new road, following the direction of the ancient roadway, have brought to light specimens of antique pottery and what appears to have been the solid pavement of the once populous city. Pella does not seem, however, to have been very extensive as the capital of a kingdom; it is supposed by one author to have reckoned three miles in circumference, though it is called at the same time a 'splendid city'! Philip was the first to make of it a place of importance.

Several large tumuli may be remarked in the surrounding country, two of them very near to the little village; they are supposed by Colonel Leake to be tombs of some of the noble families of Macedonia.

We remained for several hours at the khan of Pella, which, like most buildings of the sort, is a rambling tenement round a square courtyard, the ground-floor devoted to the stabling, the floor above, composed of little cell-like chambers, opening on a broad wooden balcony.

We did not enter the building on this occasion, but in the following year, once more on the way towards Monastir, we, my brother and myself, escorted and guarded by the head cavass of the British Consulate, overtaken by a violent storm as we drew near to this spot, were obliged to take refuge and pass the night at this desolate khan of Pella; the accommodation is such as is usually to be found in these parts, and deserves a few words of description.

It is nearly dark as, drenched with rain, weary and hungry, we stop at the gateway and summon the khandji or guardian of this splendid house of entertainment. After some delay he appears in a ragged caftan and tattered sheepskin cloak. Alarmed, probably, at the appearance of foreigners, he declares that there are no rooms, that the staircase is broken down, that it is quite impossible to receive us. We insist. Is there not a ladder? It must be managed, for we are going to stay.

The old bundle of sheepskins totters off and eventually brings a small ladder, which proves on trial to be too short to reach the top of the crumbling wall, the first plateau of the ascent; there is a struggle, a gymnastic effort, a dread lest the large stone should give way under your grasp, and you find yourself kneeling on the summit; but there is a further elevation to be attained—a wooden platform still higher up. You seize a beam on the right, a friendly hand grasps your left shoulder, and you are landed, but not yet in safety; a yawning chasm at your feet, in the rotten flooring of the gallery, warns you to look carefully to every step.

The khandji, with a tiny brush, is raising a cloud of dust in a small cell close by—he is making your room comfortable; the floor and the walls of this luxurious chamber are of mud; there is an unglazed window, a fireplace, and no ceiling; through the black rafters overhead you catch glimpses of the starlit heavens, for the storm has cleared off. The khandji brings in a tattered mat, an earthen pitcher of water, a lighted brazier of charcoal is hoisted with considerable difficulty up the wall, on to the platform outside your door, and you are left alone to your own devices.

Now, if you are experienced, you will know that there is much resource in the flat top of a small travelling-bag, that the pile of cloaks makes a comfortable seat, and that an egg stands majestically in the scooped out hollow of a piece of bread. You have brought with you provisions from the last town, including tea, sugar, and a spirit-lamp. The khandji will furnish you with coffee, and perhaps some milk; but if he should offer to sell you a salad ready dressed, avoid it; the lamp and the lettuce have an equal interest in the contents of the oil-can.

I found that a thin mattress spread on the earthen floor has at least the advantage of not being rickety, and I may have slept for some hours, when I awoke with a start: a cat rushing through the open window—which in default of glass had not even a shutter—had thrown down the cloak fastened against the opening, so that I remained gazing out into the moonlight upon the ancient fountain and the ruin on the hill above; swallows were flying in and out, building their nests and quarrelling, and a large jackdaw, with his head on one side, gravely contemplated me from the railing of the gallery in front.

The next day we thought ourselves happy in having met with no other interruption, when we learnt that it is considered very unsafe to stop at Pella: the neighbouring village is a nest of brigands.

VODENA.

THE daylight is fading as we draw near to the foot of the mountain. For the last few miles the country had become slightly undulating; clumps of trees began to appear, at first few and far between, then in thick masses of foliage, until, as we passed carefully along the uneven remains of the old Via Egnatia, we reached a firm, broad road winding through a perfect garden of the richest cultivation; through orchards, vineyards, fields of Indian corn, and groves of mulberry-trees; here and there stately poplars, shooting up from the rounded clumps of walnut, chestnut, beech and oak, remind us that we have taken leave of the cypress, and that, in its stead, the poplar becomes more and more common as you approach the frontiers of Albania.

We are bound for Vodena, a considerable town that occupies the site of Ægea or Edessa, once the capital of Macedonia and the home of Alexander the Great. At length, after many a turn and winding through lanes bordered by vineyards and overarching hedgerows, the lights of Vodena shine out like stars from the summit of the high rock, and are lost as we enter a deep cutting and begin to climb in utter darkness an almost perpendicular roadway. But flitting lights draw near: the Archbishop's Albanian servants with lanterns, which, aided by the glimmer of their white fustanelles, suffice to guide us. Entering Vodena, the plunging and stumbling common to all progress through an Eastern city commences, and, giving up any attempt to guide my horse in the uncertain light, I concentrate my attention on the projecting roofs of the bazaars, which are so low that the utmost care is needed to avoid striking the head against the beams; but no misadventure occurring, we reach at length the comfortable shelter of the Archbishop's palace.

Our host waited at the foot of the stairs to welcome us, and with remarkable ease of manner and dignified courtesy conducted our worn and weary party into his reception-room, from which, after the usual compliments and coffee, he disappeared, and was soon perceived through a side window anxiously directing a bevy of young priests in laying out the supper-table in the adjoining hall.

A very elaborate and excellent supper it proved to be: fish, fresh from the neighbouring streams; fowls cooked in various ways; stewed and roast lamb; vegetables; an abundance of creamy milk and rice, and 'yaourt,' the curdled milk so much eaten throughout the East. There were cool peaches from the archiepiscopal garden, and delicate grapes from the sunny slopes of the neighbouring mountains; wines of the country and wheaten bread; but the greatest luxury of all was the delightful sensation of freshness and repose in the lulling sound of falling water; cascades were rushing under the windows; it was an exquisite relief after the long journey across the burning, sandy plain of the Vardar.

The beauty of this situation has been very much vaunted; everyone in these parts—the least enthusiastic individual, the matter-of-fact trader, or very unimaginative Jew merchant—warms into enthusiasm when he speaks of Vodena; and yet, the glorious panorama spread out in the freshness

VODENA.

To face p. 148.

of the morning made all description tame and insufficient.

The Archbishop's palace stands on the extreme verge of a high projecting spur of the mountain, which ends abruptly with a perpendicular fall. Far below, masses of walnut-trees, chestnuts and mulberry plantations, vineyards and fields of maize, spread a rich carpet of such luxuriant vegetation that the eye seems to bathe and revel in its freshness. Far and wide beyond stretches the plain of the Vardar, softened by a delicate blue haze, and in the extreme distance, a thread of silver light—the Gulf of Salonica. To the right, relieved against the blue, lilac, and gray masses of the majestic Pindus, stands out a dark projecting cliff, half hidden in a tangled wilderness of wild vines and creepers, shrubs and trees of every kind, the dashing water appearing here and there, tumbling and leaping from the rock, until lost in the green maze below, its presence still betrayed by the denser tone of the foliage, or by the rustic bridge in the bowery lane.

On the left hand the fall of the cliff is less precipitous. On the summit is an irregular collection of picturesque cottages, with dark brown or red roofs and whitewashed overhanging upper stories, and linen fluttering in the breeze from the open balconies. A steep path cut in the cliff descends like a staircase into the valley; it is enlivened occasionally by some lounging Albanian, whose brilliant scarlet jacket, white fustanelle, and long gun glitter in the sunlight, or by the less attractive but more industrious Greek or Bulgarian peasant, bearing on his head, or pushing forward on a donkey, masses of green mulberry leaves for the silkworms reared in the cottages above. The mountains, which on this side approach nearer, and have a softer slope, are covered, some way up, with woods and vineyards, villages and white country houses, masses of plane-trees, fountains and 'kiefs.'

There are few apparent remains of antiquity in this ancient capital of Macedonia; some ruins of a wall of very ancient date, and what are supposed to be the foundations of a small temple, can be seen amongst the pomegranate-trees that fringe the edge of the cliffs. There is also a curious old church attached to the Archbishop's palace, with columns surmounted by richly ornamented capitals, one of them beautifully sculptured with rams' heads and fore-feet, another finely worked in a design of stags' heads and hoofs.

The name of Vodena, derived from the Bulgarian word 'voder' (water), is truly descriptive of this spot, where running water forms the principal feature of the locality; it rushes headlong down the middle of all the streets, gushing out in copious fountains at every turn; and, finally, bounding over into the plain in many a wild cascade, runs impetuously under each rustic bridge, until, with the name of the Kara Asmak (anciently the Lydias), it passes by Pella, trickles through the plain, and wasting its feeble strength in the marshes that border the Gulf of Salonica, reaches the sea at last, an insignificant streamlet.

OCHRIDA, AND THE MONASTERY OF ST. NAUM.

THE situation of Ochrida is one of the most beautiful in this land of picturesque beauty—the lake district of Western Turkey, on the borders of Albania. The city rose into importance in the reign of Justinian, when Lychnidus, on the eastern shore of the lake, was destroyed by earthquake. Justinian, a native of these parts, endowed Ochrida with churches, which remain to this day, though partly fallen to ruin. Two of these, the Metropolitan Church and St. Sophia, are remarkable for the great amount of fresco painting with which they are lined. In the latter the walls, roof, galleries, staircase, crypt, all exhibit the industry, and, sometimes, the skill of the artist; not an inch of space is left unemployed, and the building is very large.

The Metropolitan Church, on the contrary, is small; it is ornamented throughout in the same

OCHRIDA.

To face p. 152.

manner, but in a better style of art; an inscription on the gallery, in Greek, states that 'Pictures are specially used as a means of religious instruction to the tribes of the Mœsians.' On this subject we find in the 'Manuel d'Iconographie Chrêtienne' that 'Pauselinos of Thessalonica was commissioned to paint the Metropolitan Church of Ochrida.' It was this same Pauselinos who determined the character and types of Greek ecclesiastical art, which remain practically unchanged down to the present time. He is supposed to have lived in the reign of Andronicus I.; some ancient frescoes are shown as his work in the principal church of Karies on Mount Athos.

From the steep descent of the western slopes of the Pindus you may look down upon the beautiful lake, and upon the ancient city, covering, with its crumbling, battlemented walls and fortress, its ruined palaces, its old cathedral, and rambling wooden dwellings, a high promontory at the northern extremity; on the western shore, the long range of the Albanian mountains, piled in sublime confusion, crowned by the snow-capped peaks above Dibra, Elbassan, and Berat; in the southern distance a faint outline of lofty summits marks the position of Janina; while beneath, on the border of the lake, a bright speck like the sparkle of a diamond points out the monastery of St. Naum.

St. Naum is six hours south of Ochrida, and being quite out of the direct road usually followed by the tourists crossing to the Adriatic, has been very rarely visited by Europeans. Our small party divided, some preferring the water route, while the horses were sent round by the picturesque bridle-path skirting the lake; it passes through a thick forest where may still be found, they say, some remains of the ancient capital, once an important station on the Egnatian Way.

Our cavalcade was led by Hussein, the Consul's Albanian cavass, and by a crimson-clad suridji acting as guide, and followed by Black Saïd, shouting and vociferating to the baggage horses in his charge.

We crossed the Sook-sou with water up to the horses' girths, and followed the narrow track along beautifully shaded lanes, between hedgerows heavy with their perfumed maze of blossoms, until, after two hours of quick riding, we stopped to rest at a little village near the supposed site of the ruins of Lychnidus, already mentioned. But I sought in vain for vestiges of antiquity: the thick mantle of foliage that covers the face of the mountain makes such research almost impossible: my Albanians, quite satisfied with the positive comfort of a lump of black bread and a pinch of tobacco, had small sympathy for speculative research, and I resigned myself to the contemplation of the grotesque attire of the worthy housewives who stopped to stare at our group on their way to the village fountain. They wear a monstrous girdle of black goat's hair, with a large square of thick stuff, rigid with embroidery and gold thread, hanging from the shoulders like a breast-plate put on behind; it ends in a fringe of goat's-hair tails reaching to the feet.

The road on leaving this place enters a thick forest, crossing a steep spur of the mountain; it is very rugged and difficult, a mere horse-track, disappearing in a shelving slope at the head of the gullies, and it was necessary to moderate the ardour of Hussein, who, judging the locality singularly suited to the execution of a wild sort of Albanian 'fantasia,' was dashing along, throwing his arms up, brandishing his gun and shrieking with excitement.

At the Durbend everyone dismounted, and went down the winding staircase of rock on foot, until once again skirting the lake ; then at a smart canter through fields and grassy glades, over a gray stone bridge, to the foot of the paved road winding upwards to the monastery.

Here we paused a moment : the suridji, quite unused to such rapid locomotion, was panting behind, vainly endeavouring, by a ponderous amble, to assert his dignity as leader and guide of the party. Travellers in the East are expected to conform to the foot-pace of the baggage animals, or at least not to exceed the rahwan or amble, when the horses can accomplish it ; but trotting is almost unknown, and as to the gallop, such precipitancy is only pardonable in tatars and couriers with despatches, or wild spirits careless of propriety. The disconcerted guide was now allowed to take his proper place, followed by Hussein, and with all becoming solemnity our little procession passed through the vaulted archway of St. Naum.

The speck which had glittered so brightly in

MONASTERY OF ST. NAÚM.

To face p. 156.

the distance had taken form and substance as the windings of the road brought us within nearer view of the monastery. It was not a white building, after all, but a bewildering mass of dark-gray moss-covered stone, brown rafters, projecting balconies and sloping roofs, with just enough whitewash in the upper story to pick out and intensify the rich tone of the old timbers. To add that, standing as it does on a projecting tongue of land, all this is mirrored in the clear water of a little bay; that it is backed by forest-clad mountains overtopped by snowy peaks, can give but a faint idea of the exquisite beauty of the picture, the vigorous colouring of the old monastery with its groves and gardens, and the pearly tints of the distant range rising from the shores of the Adriatic.

A great clanging of bells greeted our arrival; it proceeded from one large bell, a piece of metal struck with a mallet and a wooden bar; the din was terrific. I was glad to escape by following a bearded monk up a wooden exterior staircase and through rambling ante-chambers, into a large, well-furnished room overhanging the lake. Here, comfortably established in the corner of the divan,

I could look down from one window on the mazy windings of a small river, green with the deep shadowing of its leafy canopy; from the other side of the angle I could see far over the liquid plain to the distant crags and wild fastnesses of Albania, or watch our little boat, with its white awning, making way steadily forwards to the monastery.

The prior, the Reverend Father Seraphim, fat, good-humoured, and hospitable, came to offer his compliments of welcome. He seemed very willing to be chatty: the visit of European ladies was an event till then unknown in the annals of that remote nook, and his inquiries, accompanied and modified by the usual refreshments of sweet-meats and coffee, lasted until the arrival of the rest of the party. They were in high spirits, and quite ready for dinner after the long row; but this proved far too important a business to be hurried. Elaborate preparations were being made; hour after hour we waited, the gentlemen making from time to time sallies of inspection, and returning to report slow and solemn progress, until, near ten o'clock at night, we were invited to the table.

The crockery and all the things supposed to be

necessary to the reception of a Frank party had been brought with great trouble from Ochrida; we saw again the familiar 'willow pattern'; there were knives, forks, and drinking glasses. The merry old prior served each dish himself, now and then employing his finger to assist the operation; perhaps it was for the first time that he used a knife and fork, but he managed it very well upon the whole. During the repast he shook with laughter as he related many a droll anecdote, and told long stories of his forced reception of large bodies of military passing through the province. His anxieties had not, however, made him thin; doubtless he kept himself well up with the generous produce of the rich vineyards of the monastery, always at hand.

The community of St. Naum, formerly composed of fifty or sixty monks, now numbers only five or six. The monastery was built in the ninth century, by St. Naum, who was one of the 'Mission of Seven' sent by the Greek Church for the conversion of the Bulgarians to Christianity.

The two principal members of this missionary band—the brothers Cyril and Methodius, sons of a patrician family of Thessalonica—undertook a task of immense difficulty, it being necessary to arrange an alphabet and found a written language, in order to translate and explain the Holy Scriptures. History states that they converted a large proportion of the Bulgarian people, and, finally, the King, Bogaris, to the Christian faith; he was baptized by the name of Michael, then Emperor of Constantinople, A.D. 861.

Amongst the members of the 'Mission of Seven'—all of whose names have been preserved—we find those of St. Clement and St. Naum as founders of this monastery; the latter undertaking more particularly the construction of the edifice; some stones in one part of it are pointed out as remains of the palace of King Michael (Bogaris). The tomb of St. Clement is shown near one of the ruined palaces of Ochrida.

This monastery is a place of reception for pilgrims, merchants, and traders, who pass through in considerable numbers during the year. An orphan asylum, containing on an average sixty orphans, is attached to the establishment. It is also much resorted to for the cure of lunatics, who are brought here from distant parts of the country. The patients are subjected to a very peculiar treatment, the same method being employed, without discrimination, in every case. During forty days they are kept in strict confinement, and fed on bread and vinegar, administered once in the twenty-four hours. The most important part of the remedy, however, consists in the patients being brought out each day, to sit for a certain length of time on the tomb of St. Naûm, while a portion of the Holy Gospels is read to them. The monks assert that this simple treatment never fails (!).

Tradition says that some sacrilegious persons, endeavouring to break open the tomb of the saint, in a search for concealed treasure, were struck with madness. This tomb is placed in a small side-chapel of the monastery, which stands in the centre of the great court, the only remnant of the original building. It is painted throughout with scenes from the life of St. Naûm; one picture tells that as he was conveying stones to the spot, in a cart, a lion and a bear made a sociable meal of one of the oxen, and, in punishment, were forced to submit to be themselves harnessed.

The monastery is very large; it contains a vast number of rooms and cells of different degrees, some comfortably furnished with divans and rugs. Most of the better rooms are built and fitted up by charitable persons, villages or communities, and are called by their names. In addition to the lodgings within the buildings, there are long rows of cells surrounding an outer court; these shelter, indiscriminately, people of the lower orders, drovers and their cattle.

At the time of the festival of St. Naûm, June 20, an immense concourse of people assemble in and around the monastery, and, uniting profit with piety, they hold a great fair, where much business is transacted between the upper and lower provinces.

At a very short distance from the monastery, a gush of water, several yards broad, issues from beneath a rock, and winding for a short space through a green maze of overhanging boughs, falls into the lake with sufficient force to turn a large water-wheel on the brink. This is the source of the Black Drin; it runs through the lake of Ochrida—as the Rhine and the Rhone traverse the lakes of Constance and Geneva—and issuing on the northern shore near the Albanian town of Struga, flows northwards towards the confines of Servia; then, turning to the south-west, falls into the Adriatic at a short distance below Dulcigno.

The Black Drin is remarkable as yielding salmon and salmon-trout. There is a very important fishing station at Struga, where both these fish and eels are taken in great quantities, especially the latter, a haul of 6,000 okes having been made at one time; they are salted and sent to Constantinople, Servia, and Roumania. The eels are taken in wicker traps, and the salmon speared. The fishing season lasts during May and June, and the fisheries of Struga are at that time a favourite resort of the inhabitants of Ochrida, who go there for very elaborate and recherché fish dinners.

The silver filigree work, so much in use throughout Albania, forms the chief industry of the little town of Struga; it is carried to perfection also in Ochrida, where it is in great demand for the innumerable buttons required for the adornment of both men and women, as well as for the gigantic clasps worn by Greeks and Bulgarians.

Ochrida carries on a considerable trade in furs,

which are received from Leipsic and here made up into the heavy coats so universally worn by both men and women, at all seasons of the year. To preserve the skins from moth, they simply expose them to a thorough draught, and for this purpose the ground-floor of the dwelling of a fur merchant is left clear so as to permit a free current of air; it is fitted with swinging beams. The people of Ochrida declare that this simple plan never fails in its preservative effect.

The embroidery of the splendid costumes of Albanian ladies of the better class also gives much occupation; the work is done entirely by men. A description of this dress, contributed by an eyewitness, shows it to be infinitely richer and more picturesque than the costume of Turkish ladies. The scene was the harem of the Mudir of Ochrida, then living in the old palace of Jellaleddin Bey:

'We found the hanum standing by a fountain in the court, with the skirts of her antary tucked up, helping her maidens to wash linen; she came forward, smiling, and not at all dismayed at being caught in such a homely occupation, and begging us to follow one of her women, soon after made her appearance, with her long train sweeping the ground in the most approved style. The room in which we were received was a vast chamber, divided from the great entrance-hall (in the centre of which were the remains of a handsome marble fountain) by a row of carved wooden pillars, supporting cross-beams richly ornamented with arabesque work; the ceiling of dark oak was also carved, as well as the high conical screen of the chimney.

'Eminé hanum was pretty, with a fair complexion, blue eyes, and light auburn hair. Her throat was adorned with a thick string of pearls, beside several rows of gold coins; her antary and shalvers were made of light-coloured silk, striped with gold.

'Presently another visitor arrived—an Albanian Moslem lady, residing in the neighbourhood. She entered the room completely enveloped in a large black feradjé, which, contrary to the usual custom, she retained on perceiving strangers; but afterwards, at our request, she suffered it to be taken off by her attendants, and stood upright for a few minutes before us, quite dazzling from the splendour of her attire. Over a chemisette of delicate striped gauze, richly embroidered in gold, she wore a black velvet waistcoat stiff with gold galloon, and edged with a thick row of pendant buttons in gold filigree; upon this a jacket of plum-coloured silk, also trimmed with gold, having sleeves of a peculiar form peaked at the wrists. She wore no antary, but her voluminous trousers of white striped muslin were heavily embroidered with gold. This brilliant costume was completed by a sleeveless pelisse, reaching to the feet, in crimson velvet, thickly braided with the same precious metal; a magnificent shawl girdle and a pale yellow handkerchief to confine the rippling masses of her jet-black hair. This daughter of Albania was in every respect a remarkable contrast to her Turkish hostess, as she leaned back on the cushions of the divan, lightly holding an amber-tipped tchibouk.'

RECOLLECTIONS OF MITYLENE.

I HAD long wished to visit the island of Mitylene, and at length a favourable opportunity occurring, I left Constantinople by the Austrian steamer, taking with me an old and valued servant, a native of that place, who had not returned to his home for several years.

We had made a pause at the Dardanelles, and in the course of the day passed Tenedos, which —its good wine notwithstanding—is a bare and barren-looking island, with a range of weird and desolate windmills breaking the ungraceful skyline. Seen above Imbros, the high mountain summit of Samothrace, pale and dove-coloured, melts in the soft haze of the approaching sunset.

As we turned southwards, the beautiful silhouette of the island of Mitylene gradually took clearer form and colour: a range of mountains strongly marked by ravines and deep valleys rose behind a bold rocky promontory covered by the battlemented walls of an immense fortress that extends quite down to the shore. Rounding this, the town of Mitylene (called by the natives Castro) comes in sight, and the steamer drops its anchor in the open roadstead in front of the harbour, which it cannot enter, for long neglect has made this refuge useless for vessels of any size. In stormy weather it often indeed happens that the boats of the Lloyd's and Egyptian lines simply slacken speed without anchoring; there is a record of an unfortunate merchant, a passenger for Mitylene, who could not even disembark, and was carried three or four times past his native island, between Smyrna and Stamboul. The embarking and unloading of cargo is a perilous service, and the boatmen of the great lighters, who are brought up from boyhood to brave these dangers, display an almost incredible amount of strength and skill.

There was ample time while waiting on the deck to look around. Parched, rocky, and arid as are all these islands of the Archipelago on their southern shores, the parts that face the coast of Asia Minor, sheltered from the burning westerly

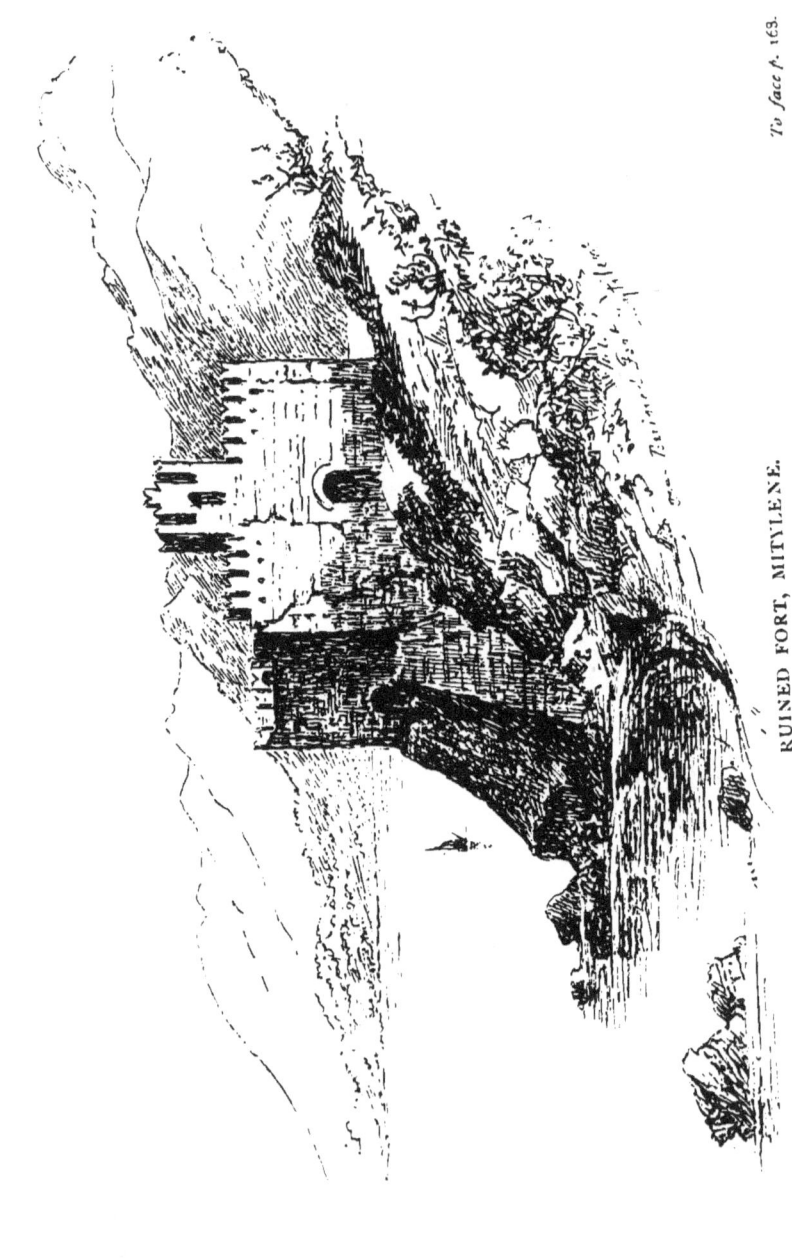

RUINED FORT, MITYLENE.

rays, and from the withering south-west gales, are luxuriantly rich and fertile.

The town of Mitylene covers an isthmus, and on this side creeps up the lower slopes of the promontory, crowned by the vast fortifications of the Genoese castle already seen from the northern side—a majestic assemblage of immense towers and bastions within two lines of high crenellated walls. Until lately a square, castellated tower, partly ruined (and now destroyed), stood on the shore at the foot of the great castle; it formed an exquisite foreground object to a picture of marvellous beauty: the bold sweep of the bay, backed by a range of mountains covered almost to the summit with luxuriant forest growth or soft pastoral cultivation; the dark green of the orange grove, contrasting with the pale, tender tone of the olive, and with the bright freshness of vineyards, meadows and upland pastures; higher still a wilderness of oak and beech and chestnuts, the whole dotted with white villages with their church steeples—with hamlets and solitary farms. Beyond the last point of the mountain range that descends in a gradual slope to the sea-shore, you can trace in the haze of distance the delicate, almost ethereal, outline of the island of Schio, and on the opposite shore the entrance to the Gulf of Smyrna.

I remained in Mitylene for several weeks, and had thus an opportunity of seeing and studying much that can scarcely come within the observation of the passing tourist. My notes of that visit date, it is true, from some years back, but since that time the natural advantages of this beautiful island, its great fertility, its numerous hot springs and mineral baths, its fine air and healthy climate, the magnificent harbours of Kaloní and Hiëra, continue unchanged; new financial and commercial enterprises have increased its wealth and importance, but the remains of ancient works and monuments, in which Lesbos, the rival of Athens, was richer than any of the islands of the eastern Archipelago, have—in many cases within these few years—been dispersed or destroyed; it seems well, therefore, to keep some record of them as they were seen in their former positions.

One of the most interesting of these relics is the chair of Potamon, son of Lesbonax, called by the natives the 'Throne'; it stands in the entrance court of the Archbishop's palace, and is used at the close of the Easter festival, when the prelate takes his seat thereon, distributes the Easter eggs to the crowd, and drinks to their health and prosperity.

This beautiful relic of the ancient splendours of Lesbos is formed of one block of white marble; one side of it is partly broken away, but the other, on the left hand, shows very elaborate sculpture; the seat is supported on the limbs and claws of a griffin; the upper part displays in high relief the entire form of the winged creature, with the exception of the head; the lower part is ornamented by a monstrous scaly serpent, that winds about a supporting column and reaches its head nearly to the marble seat : a finely carved marble footstool stands in front between the claws. The inscription on the chair says : 'The chair of Potamon, son of Lesbonax.' This Lesbonax, a native of Mitylene, lived in the time of Augustus; he was a learned man and a philosopher, and wrote several political orations, of which two only have been preserved. Potamon, his son, was a teacher of rhetoric at Rome, where he was much befriended by Tiberius. The passport written by this Emperor for Potamon, when the latter desired to return to his native island, was strongly to the point ; it ran thus: 'This is Potamon, son of Lesbonax ; if anyone dare to do him harm, let him first consider whether he be strong enough to make war upon me.'

We paid a visit to the Archbishop, who received us with a courteous welcome, and gave us of the best of sweetmeats and coffee, but I grieve to say that he showed the very faintest appreciation of the value of the historical remains over which he might—were he so inclined—exercise a preservative control.

In the immediate neighbourhood of a hospital, founded and endowed by a rich inhabitant of the city, a row of massive pediments, at regular distances, are said to be remains of the great Temple of Apollo ; several broken shafts of immense fluted columns lie amongst a tangle of weeds ;* close to these remains of a colonnade or portico, and in the neglected garden of the hospital two or three singularly beautiful capitals might seem to justify the belief of the natives that much more extensive and important ruins, with

---

* These columns have since been taken to ornament the portico of a college for boys, built on this spot.

remnants of tessellated pavement, lie beneath the surface: a rough sort of little chapel has been built on the ground, thus rendering it a sacred spot, a protection which the Mussulman population invariably respect.

The same device has been used to preserve the ruins of an ancient church or temple on the slope of the hill beyond the town; little remains to identify these ruins except blocks of marble of great size, and a few detached Greek letters on some stones; these fragments were disclosed by the displacement of the ground during the earthquake of 1867. Below this, and apparently in connection with it, a large excavation may be seen from which many blocks of marble and columns had been lately taken: some call these the ruins of a theatre.

The whole of this hill-side, leading up to the Téké, or Mussulman burial-ground, is covered with fragments of antiquity: bits of old marble and brickwork and of glazed pottery; tiny terracotta heads (of which I possess one—an exquisite head of an infant); morsels—fragments—which are nothing—but yet everything!—bearing their silent testimony to the former importance of this ancient Lesbos — the island beloved of Apollo—the resting-place of the head and lyre of Orpheus ; the birthplace of Arion ; the cradle of lyric poetry; the home of Sappho, of her friend Alceus, and of her pupil, Erinna ; the island which, ten centuries before the Christian era, was one of the richest and most prosperous in the Ægean Sea—the now almost unknown Mitylene!

The old town, indeed, particularly the Turkish quarter, which is, they say, the site of the ancient city, is full of these unconscious witnesses: every courtyard, the corners in the narrow lanes, show fragments of columns, or of sculptured capitals; here, a mass of red granite ; there, a line of delicate frieze-work let into the basement of some humble dwelling. One small church, St. George's, has its wooden portico supported on reversed columns, with exquisite Corinthian capitals. The same design is repeated in a piece of friezework with a long inscription let into a wall immediately adjoining.

Some well-preserved mosaic pavement was shown in the entry of a small house at the foot of the Castle Hill ; some other was pointed out as belonging to part of an ancient bath, near the shore, but this last has been greatly obliterated by sea deposit, and close to this spot the remains of two great moles, formerly enclosing a spacious harbour, may be traced at the base of the promontory.

We started one morning to visit the fortress, taking a little pathway through fields of green corn, where children—in preparation for the next day—May 1 (o.s.), were busy in collecting large bunches of poppies and other field flowers, to make the garlands which will be found suspended over every—even the poorest—entrance door.

Passing onwards and upwards, the little path wound through a large fig plantation; some of the trees had bunches of figs tied together, hung on their branches. It was explained that these bunches were wild figs. They are tied on to the cultivated trees in order to encourage the good fruit not to fall off!

We reached the castle; a vast bewildering enclosure chiefly encircling an extraordinary mass of fallen columns, capitals—fragments of past splendour everywhere. It was difficult, at first, in this maze of towers and battlements, more or less ancient and ruinous, to make out exactly where the garrison might be located: a koulouk, or guard-house, occupies a small, half-ruined Byzantine chapel ; but the church mentioned in a former ' Murray ' is an utter ruin ; for this, as for part of the destruction noticed on every side, neglect and carelessness are not solely responsible ; much of it is due to the terrible earthquake shocks of 1867.

Within the wall of the fortress there exists a large ancient cistern ; a part of one fluted shaft of a column still stands in the water, but the roof is now supported on several columns, placed across like beams ; they, doubtless, formerly sustained a vaulted covering in the usual manner.

The climate of Mitylene is one of the healthiest in the East ; the mountains covered by forests of pine, and the fresh sea-breezes perfumed by the masses of aromatic plants that clothe all the uncultivated lands; the abundance of running waters, and the numerous and valuable mineral springs, combine to render this beautiful island a happy land of plenty and peace.

Extreme poverty is unknown ; most of the

inhabitants possess their own 'vines and fig-trees,' and, one may add, their fruitful and lucrative orange plantations and olive groves. The olive forms not the only, but the principal source of wealth of the inhabitants; it may be said to absorb their every thought. 'I know many men here,' said my host, 'who are immensely rich; they do not at all enjoy their wealth, they have neither fine houses nor comfortable furniture; they have little education, and no ideas; their only thought is to gaze up, heads thrown back, and open-mouthed, into their olive trees, asking themselves, "Will there be a good crop of olives this season?"'

There is, however, one thing to be said in favour of the poor rich men: that in all the schools of the island education is gratuitous, maintained entirely by the inhabitants: every man is obliged, according to his means, if not by law, at least by established custom, to contribute very liberally, and to leave money in his will for schools and hospitals.

Looked upon as a Greek country under Turkish rule (the larger proportion of the inhabitants being Greek), Mitylene may be considered to hold a high rank, in the matter of public instruction;

the college of Castro deems itself to be superior to that of Smyrna.

A very lively import and export trade is carried on here, an interchange of goods and manufactures between Europe and Asia. Some of these exports are not quite familiar to the English stranger. For instance, among the long list of wine and oil, soaps, potteries, valonea acorns, wools and hides, there are the great leather skins, used throughout the East for holding wine, oil, flour, etc.

Wandering one day through the principal business street of Castro, I was amused and interested to observe the primitive and practical way of testing these skins. Every hole being of course closed, the skin, which looks like a skinned animal minus the head, is inflated by a bellows; when quite full of air, a man gives it a tremendous blow, and, if sound, it is laid aside for future use. In this instance they were preparing them for holding the oil to be employed in the soap manufactories.

This is a very busy, industrious town, and a great amount of its interest is centred in oil and soap; therefore, after seeing the skins duly banged and tested, we stepped a few yards further on, into the premises of a soap manufactory, to look at the great oil-presses worked by steam. An improvement on the primitive method was introduced some years since, by English merchants from Smyrna, who own a large establishment, where the refuse from the oil mills—formerly cast away—is utilized and made to yield a considerable amount of greenish oil, by means of hydraulic pressure. In the immediate neighbourhood of these works, excavations on the hillside have brought to light funereal urns and other remains of an ancient necropolis.

But to return to the 'tcharshi,' which is even more interesting than the market-place of a Western city; for here, in the East, not only the produce of the country, the strange fruits, and unaccustomed wares, the costume of the peasantry and the life of the place are to be seen, but the manufacture of almost every article is carried on in public, in the open shops. You may watch the 'cadaïf' sprinkled from a small funnel on to the heated disc; it dries, curls, separates, and in a few minutes a hank of the delicate vermicelli-like article is ready for sale. You may overlook, if so inclined, the genuine preparation of 'kebabs' from the very beginning of the cuts from the carcase, hanging in a convenient cool corner, or, passing on, pause again to wonder at the rapidity and care with which rahat lokoum, sugared almonds, candies and sweets innumerable, are produced. The next shop, perhaps, is devoted to milk; people are sitting there, at rough tables, eating their bread and milk, helped out of great pans, with ladles, which are simply the half of a gourd, with its long stick-like natural handle. On the open shop-front are ranged bowls of 'mohalibé,' rice-flour and milk, sprinkled with sugar and rose-water, finished with lumps of clotted cream, in the proper season; other bowls, of 'aschourah,' a mystic and symbolical mixture of ten substances; 'ekmek cadaïf,' very thin pancakes, with lumps of clotted cream inserted; and so on, through an endless variety of sweet confections.

In the herb shop you will find, amongst many familiar dried plants and herbs, the 'origanum,' (wild marjoram), called by the natives 'rhigani,' the blossom of a low shrub growing wild in great profusion all over the uncultivated land; it has somewhat the scent of thyme; an oil is extracted from it, which is used in medicine, and exported to Germany and Austria.

Another article, which instead of being exported is, on the contrary, imported from Athens, Venice, the Danube, and many other places, may seem extraordinary to those who look here upon mountains covered with the finest forest growth of pinewoods—planks and wood for house-building of the better class. The splendid forest growth is used for inferior dwellings, for firewood, and perhaps for ship-building ; but an unpleasant peculiarity about these pine-trees (not unknown elsewhere), and that is especially prevalent in the neighbourhood of Kalonì—is the objectionable fact, that the tree itself breeds bugs to such an extent that anyone endeavouring to rest in the grateful shade is immediately aware of this repulsive and most undesirable circumstance.

The Mityleniotes are a fine race, the men tall and well made. Their proper costume (which is, alas ! rapidly yielding to the mean and ungraceful outlines of Western civilization) consists of a short cloth jacket worn open, and displaying a highly fashionable waistcoat, open nearly to the waist ; a gorgeous scarf, wound loosely ; extremely full and ample trousers—the mass of superfluous folds, swaying heavily with every step, reaches nearly to the ground; but the crowning peculiarity consists of polished leather shoes, very square in the toes, and made expressly about four inches longer than the foot, that they may crinkle and turn up becomingly.

The women of Mitylene, in ancient times so celebrated for their beauty, their wit and fascination, and their skill in needlework and embroidery, often combine the charm of wavy auburn or dark hair and long lashes with eyes of bluish-gray; delicate features, and an upright and firm carriage, as though fully impressed with their great social importance—and not without reason, for, in Mitylene, owing to exceptional circumstances, the custom arose in the fifteenth century of giving the greatest advantages to the daughters of a family, to the prejudice of the sons. It is the eldest daughter who inherits the family mansion; it is for her that the spinning-wheel and the loom are kept in activity almost from the moment of her birth, and although the younger daughters are not forgotten, it is always the eldest girl who is the favoured child of the family. Many endeavours have been made in order to equalize these somewhat unjust measures, and to give the sons their due proportion of family prosperity; but ancient custom is tenacious, and as yet little progress has been made towards a more equitable partition.

These young Lesbian maidens wear a very ample 'divided skirt,' from out of which their often bare feet contrast strangely with the elaborate adornments of jacket and waistcoat, and with the graceful muslin handkerchief used as a headdress, trimmed with its dainty silken flowers. One or two ancient dames, clinging to the fashions of their long past youth, still envelop their heads in a wonderful swathing of black muslin, topped by one gigantic bow, stiffened, square, and standing high up, so that the whole arrangement bears a curious resemblance to the helmet of Minerva, as represented in the very earliest sculptures. The natives of Mitylene imagine that this strange headdress has been handed down from that remote mythological time.

They are very industrious, and as we pass onwards the whirr of the loom or the hum of the spinning-wheel comes from many an open doorway. The looms are generally set up in the large covered yard forming the basement of the house, and many young girls, with bright flowers in their hair, are weaving the woollen stuff, or the linen, in preparation for their marriage outfit. One is irresistibly reminded of Erinna, a native of this place, and a pupil of Sappho, who died in her early youth, leaving to posterity the three hundred lines of her poem, 'The Distaff,' composed while spinning in the humble cottage of her mother, who disapproved of her gifted child's poetic fancies. She breathed out her soul to the movement of her loom, and passed away in the dawn of her genius and renown. This poem has not been preserved, but it is mentioned and highly praised by several of the poets whose lines form the Greek Anthology. The following extract (translated for me) is a specimen of one of these sonnets :

'There is a little sweet Lesbian wax of Erinna's, but it is all mixed with honey from the Muses. Her three hundred lines are equal to Homer's, and she a maiden of nineteen years ; a worshipper of the Muses, she was touching the distaff, in fear of her mother, who stood at the web.

Erinna is as far above Sappho in hexameters, as Sappho is above Erinna in lyric verses.'

In the courtyard of a mosque a hollow sarcophagus is shown as the tomb of Sappho; this relic, one would say, is more than doubtful.

THE HARBOUR OF THE OLIVES.

MITYLENE can boast of three natural harbours; the largest, that of Kalonì, is of vast extent, but the surrounding land is marshy and unhealthy : the harbour of Sigri is on the west coast : and the large inlet, the most important in the Archipelago, known as the Harbour of the Olives, sometimes also called Hiéra, is only distant about four miles from the capital; it is easily reached by one of the fine roads made several years ago by an Engineer officer in the Turkish service, General Belinski. These excellent works have suffered greatly from earthquake, and still more from subsequent want of repair. But if the way is somewhat rough and irregular, the charm of the exquisite vistas that open out with every turn of the winding ascent through mulberry plantations and olive groves, leading us steeply upwards towards the summit of the pass, would fully repay much greater exertion. On the left hand, the mountain side sweeps downwards towards the sea, covered with splendid forest growth, in which two white villages with their churches shine out like clusters of jewels in their deep green setting : here and there a solitary tchiftlik sparkles, or a group of dwellings near the foot of the mountain stands clearly defined against the soft azure of the calm water.

We pass a flock of goats sprinkled over the slope, goats of many colours, dark and fair—deep brown, coffee-coloured, dark gray, pale gray, and snowy white. They are eating with intense satisfaction the large ruby arums that grow in abundance, and that do not seem to emit, here, the unbearable odour that exhales from these plants in the plains of Broussa. The peasants all deck themselves with natural flowers, and the young goatherd, not finding a suitable blossom ready to hand, has beautified himself with a long stalk of green bearded wheat, jauntily placed over his left ear.

The road winds still upwards through sunlight and shadow, until the summit of the pass is reached, and the beautiful panorama opens out over the blue Ægean, dotted with snow-white sails; beyond, in the pale distance, the site of Pergamos is pointed out, then the coast of Magnesia, and all that wonderful roll of mountain beyond mountain, leading away into the heart of that historic land of buried cities and vanished splendour.

The road on the right hand begins to descend by a cutting amongst crags and boulders of gray rock, half buried in masses of ilex, of feathery olive and sturdy full-leaved mulberry trees. Still further, great patches of brilliantly red earth begin to appear on the high banks, and we pass a party of women and boys busily scraping it out: they will use it as paint to redden their earthen stoves.

A little further still and, far down, partly seen through a delicate veil of olive groves, the beautiful inlet, the Harbour of the Olives,* looking like a great silent lake (as the extremely narrow entrance is from here invisible), runs for fifteen miles into the land, sheltered by mountains on either side. A space of level ground, bordering the water of the opposite shore, shows a thick plantation of poplar-trees, grown in order to pro-

* More properly called the Gulf of Hiéra.

KENDROS: THE HARBOUR OF THE OLIVES.

duce the long wands necessary for knocking down the ripe olives.

At our feet we look down upon the roofs and vine-garlanded terraces of a considerable bathing establishment, built over the hot mineral springs of Kendros. There are two sources that supply these baths, and the great marble basins or tanks of ancient construction, are supposed to accommodate fifty bathers without inconvenience. These springs are situated some fifteen or twenty yards apart, but are in the same group of buildings.

Mitylene is very rich in mineral springs, the three principal sources being Kendros, Thermi, and Polichniti. This is to be expected in an island that can boast of two extinct volcanoes, one in the neighbourhood of Petra, beyond Methymna, the other near Polichniti. Volcanic rocks are found at the very gates of the city—the soil of the whole island seems, indeed, to be composed of volcanic remains; and the terrible earthquake shocks, from which Mitylene has suffered so severely, would show that if the volcanoes are now extinct, the latent power which they once developed still exists.

The hot iron springs of Polichniti are in the mountains, not far from the entrance of the Gulf of Kaloní, and at more than thirty miles distance from Castro. The heat of the water is so great, even after its exposure to the air as it flows down the mountain side, that the neighbouring villagers use it as a natural kitchen; they simply plunge their pans and kettles into the stream, and everything is cooked to perfection. I did not reach this distant spring, but in company of a friend and attended by our respective servants, I visited the baths of Thermi.

THERMI, THE GREAT CYPRESS AND THE RUINED AQUEDUCT.

WE embarked in one of the large boats used in conveying cargo and passengers for the great steamers. The morning was brilliantly fine, but there was a heavy swell, and the shape of the boat, combined with the height of the sides, caused a good deal of movement, and at the same time a very quiescent state of low spirits among our little party. The wind also was contrary, and it took us nearly an hour to round the promontory, and two more before reaching the little landing-place of Thermi, having passed two pretty white villages embosomed in olive-groves, Mauria and Pamphilia.

The baths, which are at a few minutes' walk from the shore, were crowded, chiefly with peasantry, for there is no sort of accommodation for bathers of the better class, who must find a lodging in the poor little village, and have the water brought to them with great trouble and expense. I have heard these waters spoken of as most valuable and efficacious by sufferers who had been relieved, if not quite cured, of sciatica, rheumatism, and other similar troubles, and there is no doubt that a small hotel on the spot, giving the simple comforts indispensable for an invalid, could not fail of success.

The women's bath was crowded to suffocation ; the square basin, of very ancient construction, has a roof supported on a massive fluted column with sculptured capital ; a dozen women, forming a chain, were circling round this column, singing in chorus, the water up to their necks and each head enturbaned with white towelling : in the deep gloom of the bath, which receives no light except from the small rounds of semi-opaque glass in the roof, the effect was decidedly witch-like and uncanny. Outside the part of the group of buildings assigned to the use of the men, one remarks many portions of columns and several inscriptions in ancient Greek, on slabs let into the walls.

The waters of Thermi contain iron and sulphur,

as is shown by the trickling streamlet rushing down a little gully full of bright red, yellow and green stones. In a valuable local account of the advantages and resources of Mitylene, I find the heat of this water marked at 37° centigrade, and that close by there is a spring with the taste and qualities of seltzer-water. The heat was intense, and we were glad to seek even a modified shade amongst the olive-groves on our way to one of the wonders of the island—the giant cypress-tree—following an old woman who volunteered as guide.

But the olive-trees of Mitylene, unlike those of Crete, give but a pretence of shade from the blazing sun ; the way was airless, the track rough and stony, and we had nearly abandoned the toilsome ascent, when a dark tree summit towering above the paler foliage is perceived, and we take heart; pausing only beside a rustic fountain to watch a group of Turkish women on their way to the bath, and to admire a Wallachian gipsy, whose wonderfully expressive face was strangely attractive, in spite of dirt and tatters.

We reach the tree, a truly wonderful specimen of the spreading cypress—such a trunk ! such gnarled branches! such towering dark foliage!—apparently the only one of its kind in these parts. No wonder that many legends cling about this sylvan giant. One monstrous arm had been taken off, professedly for use in the building of a church, by some man of past times, who, however, changed his mind, and using the precious wood for his own house-building, was thereafter the victim of continued misfortune to the end of his life. Another venturesome person cut off a small part of the tree, and immediately the wood began to bleed! The natives say that the great cypress-tree is as old as the world. Doubtless it saw the ancient columns of porphyry and marble, the capitals and sculptured stones—now lying about, neglected and broken—upright and each in its own place. Who knows its age? Who knows its real history?

Beyond the limits of shadow cast by the giant cypress the heat was intense; I made a conscientious and perfectly futile attempt to find a point from which a sketch might be possible; all around was too thickly wooded, and there was a secret, unconfessed feeling of relief in realizing that the proper spot is unfindable.

RUINED AQUEDUCT, MITYLENE.

To face p. 194.

We left Thermi in the cool of the evening, giving passage in the large boat to an itinerant musician, with his hand-organ. The four boatmen and my friend's two native girls, Màlama and Agnoula, are delighted. The organ wails from time to time to encourage the rowers, for we are beginning to run a race with the Egyptian steamer which is in sight; our rowers strain at the oars, the steamer begins to slacken speed; with a screeching whistle and great rattling of anchor chains, it stops in the roadstead as we turn into the harbour, and liberate our eager boatmen for their further duties.

Beyond the pretty village of Mauria, at a short distance from Mitylene towards the north, there are some noble ruins of an aqueduct, which connects the beautifully wooded sides of a valley and crosses a small stream that ripples towards the sea, half-hidden by boulders of pale gray marble and masses of blossoming white and pink oleander, of thyme-scented 'rhigani,' and aromatic plants innumerable.

It is a stately ruin, reminding one strongly of the celebrated 'Pont du Gard'; the upper tier of small arches is wanting in the Mitylene aqueduct, but it resembles it in the surrounding features of the scenery, and in the massive perfection of the masonry that still remains to show what it must have been when, some sixty or seventy years ago, it was—so say the natives—still entire ; but, alas! earthquake and ruthless destruction have sadly reduced these noble proportions, and only three tiers of the central arches continue unspoiled : earthquake began the destruction on the left side of the stream, and the owner of some land on the other bank, seeing how well these beautifully wrought stones served for building purposes, began pulling down on his side, stone by stone, until only this ruin amongst olive groves and mulberry plantations remains to keep in memory the once stately structure.

The range of arches in the upper part is of red and brown brickwork, supported on massive piers of beautifully cut, bevelled and fitted stone, in alternate courses of very large square and of oblong blocks ; there were probably twelve arches in its original length, and in the dip of the valley three, or perhaps four, arches in the foundations : the thick undergrowth of oleander, mingled with boulders of gray marble, made it difficult to ascertain correctly. This fine work appears to have conveyed water to the town, at the time when Mitylene was a splendid and important city, by a succession of gaunt pillars of masonry, some of which still remain, according to a system of waterworks said to have been imported by the Arabs; similar water-towers are still in use in Stamboul, in connection with the aqueducts and the 'bends' of Bagtchekeuy and Belgrade.

MOLIVO AND PETRA.

I PREPARED for an excursion to Molivo, the ancient Methymna, attended by our old and faithful servant Panayoti. To say that we hoped to start at a given time would be paying too great a compliment to the little coasting-steamer *Mabel*, whose wandering and erratic programme took her between Cavalla, Porto Lago, Dede Agatch, Imbros, Tenedos, Molivo, Mitylene and Smyrna, therefore we were ready, and—waited: we waited several hours beyond the time officially announced, and finally reached our destination, Molivo, by ten o'clock at night.

One large boat came alongside from the Custom House; it was soon heaped high with bales of merchandize, upon the top of which the few passengers were expected to perch, and afterwards to undergo a lengthy and vexatious examination of our very small amount of luggage.

There being nothing in the nature of a hotel at Molivo, I had been provided with a letter to a certain Kyrio Stavridès, one of the superior merchants of the place. The better part of the town is built up the precipitous slopes of the hill on which the castle stands, and, guided by a boatman, acting also as porter, who preceded us with a dusky lantern hung at the end of a stick, we began a rough and very steep ascent towards the twinkling lights that sparkled out of the darkness high above our heads. It was a frightful experience, up and up, and sometimes over, great boulders of rock.

The road seemed roughly cut in the face of a precipice, with little or no protection on the downward side; but still struggling upwards, by many a sharp turn and winding, we reach, at length, our destination, and knock at the door of a goodlooking house. Some dogs bark fiercely at this unusual clamour; it is near midnight, and at first there is no response: then louder knocks, and a girl's voice from some unseen window inquires the reason of the disturbance; afterwards a man's voice from above, and then a white-clad vision appears in the half-open doorway; he looks at the letter, says 'Welcome,' reads a second time, comprehends the situation, and with a sigh retires, to give place to the mistress of the house. All these unfortunate people have been roused from their sleep, and yet, although I am a stranger and totally unexpected, the greatest hospitality and kindness is shown most ungrudgingly; their best drawing-room is at once turned into a sleeping apartment, and poor weary Panayoti accommodated somewhere among the rooms on the ground floor.

The next morning showed a glorious view of mountains, above a fertile and beautifully cultivated plain and richly wooded slopes. The house of Stavridès, nearly on the highest part of the town, stands close to the boundary of the old Genoese castle of Molivo, built on more ancient foundations, and on a cluster of immense black crags that are the beginning of a chain of basaltic rocky heights, that extend across the island as far as Kàloni. I find it stated that some traces of the ancient walls of Methymna may be discovered on the south side of the mountain, with the ruins of a great tower and of a bath: the town of Molivo clusters on the side towards

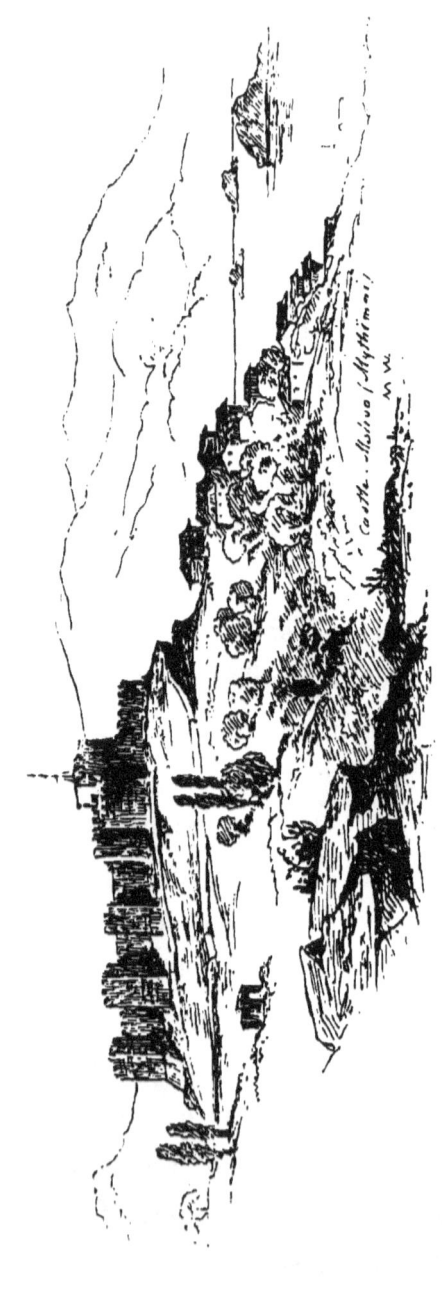

CASTLE OF MOLIVO.

the water, and at the foot of these grim volcanic rocks.

An old French cannon is shown in the enclosure of the fortress, how obtained it is not stated, but there are few vestiges of ancient Greek work; here and there merely some fragments of columns and a capital.

We descend towards the plain and, crossing a picturesque old bridge, follow the bed of a small stream bordered by oleanders, pink and white, till we reach the edge of the sands of the seashore, where masses of lilac-coloured 'everlastings,' great tufts of broom in flower amongst the crags, and a large garden near at hand full of the flame-like pomegranate blossoms, made up, with the sapphire sea for background, a quite bewildering maze of exquisite colour; above these twisted branches of pomegranate, fig, and wreathing vine, rose the great mass of the Castle summit, veiled by the haze of evening into a tender tone of violet gray, against a glowing sky of crimson and orange cloudlets, that melted as they floated away into the pure radiance of faintest green and azure.

As in duty bound, we visited the schools of

Molivo, of which there are two for boys and one for girls: the boys have the advantage of going afterwards to Athens or elsewhere for further instruction, but it seems that the education of the young maidens of Methymna is sadly rudimentary. It is doubtful if they know—or knowing, would appreciate the fact—that Arion, the celebrated lyric poet, was a native of this place, and the subsequent legend (according to local authorities) that he was borne on the back of a friendly dolphin, playing on his cithara and singing, to his home; witness a charming little painting in the Louvre (French Gallery), where the dolphin is gazing up at his unusual burden with a fervour of ecstatic delight. Then again, were not the head and the lyre of Orpheus buried somewhere between Molivo and Cape Sigri, where the lyre continued to enchant the very rocks and stones, and the head of the unhappy victim of the Thracian furies gave forth utterances of such surpassing wisdom, that even the Delphic oracles were neglected in their favour?

In these prosaic days the vines and the fig-trees of Molivo are of the highest importance; the famous Lesbian wine, so celebrated in ancient times, was especially cultivated in this district; in the present day it is esteemed as good and strong and very pure, but strangers object to the native custom of colouring it with elderberries, and of washing round the casks with strongly-scented aromatic herbs, in order, they say, to preserve it.

The figs also of Molivo are in great request; all fruit, indeed, grows in these parts in great abundance, and considerable quantities are exported from Mitylene to Constantinople and Egypt, as well as vegetables, cheese, fish of many kinds, and formerly oysters to the nearer ports.

On the other hand, wheat, barley and all bread stuffs are imported, and they receive and consume a large amount of salted food from Russia, Marseilles and the shores of the sea of Marmora.

We started the next morning very early, and on foot, for Petra, a town on the opposite side of the deep bay of Molivo. The descent into the plain was fearfully rough, but once on the high-road one could appreciate the good work that had been done there before earthquake and neglect left it ruined in many places; it was no one's business to keep it in order, therefore even the smooth way had soon to be abandoned for a stony horse-track across the mountain slope, and amongst rough crags and clusters of lilac 'everlasting,' by very rustic way-side fountains, by the ruins of a small chapel overshadowed by wild fig-trees, we made our way towards Petra. The rough path had fallen in in many places, and it was evident that a considerable subterranean passage wound along between Molivo and Petra; one frightful chasm breaking the direct line of way was especially dangerous: it was near the summit of the pass, after which we began to descend a wild cascade of rolling stones towards the shore, then by an equally painful progress among reeds and sand we reached at length the goal of our expedition, Petra.

The little town stands on the shore at the extremity of a fertile, richly-cultivated valley; the town itself is on the level of the sea, but in the centre of it rises one huge solitary mass of gray rock, surmounted and crowned by the church; in the background a noble range of mountains stretches across into the interior of the island.

The ascent to the church is by a well-kept easy stairway; here and there, to give greater width, masses of stone have been clamped on. On the platform one sees the belfry, the so-called bell consisting of a plank of sonorous wood, struck by a mallet; this method of call is still very much used in remote places throughout the East.

Two old women of some semi-religious order had charge of this rock-built church of Petra; one of them wore a black serge dress, with a leather and brass belt; she was a merry old soul. The building did not appear to be very ancient, probably of the time of the Genoese occupation, as a monumental stone, bearing the arms of the Gatelutzi, is set in the pavement of the church. The arms and emblems of this princely Genoese family are found in more than one spot in Mitylene; on a funeral slab near an ancient church, now a mosque, one may see an escutcheon and an almost effaced Latin inscription round the border; something of the same is found also on the walls of the Castle. It was at Mitylene that Constantine, the last Christian Emperor of Constantinople, espoused the daughter of Notarès

Gatelutzi, the last Christian prince of the island (1442 A.D.).

There are a few curious old paintings in this church of Petra, and a very beautiful Bishop's throne, carved in wood by a workman brought over from Aïvali, but the most remarkable feature is a well down at the base of the stupendous rock, which is reached by an awful descent of steps from the pavement; the water of it is said to be very good: it should possess some compensation for the terrible necessity of drawing it under such difficulties.

We wandered through the Tscharchi, noticing in many places the ruin caused by the last great earthquake, remarking also that the reputation of Petra for pretty women was not exaggerated, and after a long rest in the hospitable house of somebody's relation—I did not clearly make out the connection—we set out on our return laden with great bunches of the lilac 'everlastings.'

On the third morning we were to leave on our return to Mitylene by the early (?) steamer; it was announced to call at Molivo, probably at about 7 a.m.; accordingly I rose at 5.30, and waited the whole day! It was impossible to stroll out of the house lest the summons to embark should come suddenly, so the time was passed in spasmodic attempts at conversation with my kind hostess and with her mother, a very sweet-mannered, sensible old lady, who had brought with her a pet dog, a hairy little creature called Callirhoï.

Towards evening it was decided to take leave of our hosts, and to descend to the neighbourhood of the landing-place to wait for the steamer. These kind people were in a position which made a direct offer of repayment impossible (the actual outlay occasioned by my short stay may have amounted to two or three shillings), and on my urgent inquiry as to what suitable present I could send back from Constantinople, which might I hoped give them pleasure, I, with considerable difficulty, arrived at the conclusion that what my host would most willingly accept would be—a very good fowling piece!

We descended to the landing-stage, sat there a few hours, until, utterly worn out, I took refuge in an upper room of the little café, very simply furnished with a mat, and I was contemplating the probability of passing the night there, when suddenly in the street there is a great shout, a wild rushing of feet—'Ah, ah! Make haste, lady! The boat! the boat!' The boatman rushes up in intense hurry; we embark in trembling haste, to wait on board a whole hour before starting, at midnight, and to reach and land at Mitylene at dawn.

IN CRETE.

THE AKROTIRI.

A SANDY road; it is bordered on the right by gigantic aloes in full blossom; on the left by the cluster of white, flat-roofed negro dwellings, that glow in the rays of an almost tropical sunrise, in sharp relief against the azure expanse of the Mediterranean; the aloes hedge, with its mast-like flower-stalks, ceases abruptly, and the sandy level is covered with the straw and reed huts of an Arab village; Arab women and negresses pass along, balancing water-jars or large bundles on their heads; their many-coloured draperies wave in picturesque flickers about their dusky limbs, and the arm which is raised to draw together the tattered semblance of a veil is laden with bangles and tawdry bracelets; little blackies and brownies tumble amongst the sand heaps; a native of

Benghazi is following the same road with a well-dressed man from Tunis. My guide is an Italian, and the only individual of this motley group who may be fairly called a genuine native is the Cretan groom of the powerful Cyprian donkey that I am riding ; for we are in Crete, starting from Canea in the early morning of a brilliant July day to visit the caves and monasteries of the rocky headland of Cape Melec, known as Akrotiri.

I had reached the island a few weeks previously by the Austrian steamer that touches first at Rethymo, where it waits for an hour or two outside the harbour (now unusable for large vessels), and later, pauses below the massive bastion that appears to guard the once important arsenal of Candia, where the winged lion of St. Mark still clings to the crumbling wall, and some rusty, old-fashioned cannon that may have lain there—who knows ?—from the time of the Venetian occupation, are heaped beside fallen blocks of masonry on the narrow quay. In the outer harbour of Canea, the boat of the Austrian Lloyds finds, at length, but a restless and insecure anchorage.

The little African colony near which the road to Akrotiri passes was originally brought here by

Mehemet Ali of Egypt in the earlier part of this century. An attempt was made some time back to remove all the Arabs into houses of brick and stone, and much money was subscribed for the purpose, as also for the opening of a school for the benefit of the half-naked little ones ; but it is evident that the advantages of instruction are of small value in their eyes when compared with the fascinations of street puppies and mud-pies, while their parents cling to their native sand and magnified beehives, so that these well-meant efforts at civilization have been, and are likely to remain, a failure.

Leaving Africa Minor behind, we find ourselves winding upwards towards Khalépa, and, in spite of the sun, which in these Southern countries is almost as burning at its rise as at its meridian, the air is deliciously cool and bracing, scented by the thyme, myrtle, balm, basil, mint, and a multitude of aromatic plants, among which the pungent aroma of the 'lavdanum' predominates: the 'lavdanum' is a sort of cistus, yielding on the twigs and leaves a highly fragrant gum, which is collected by whipping the shrub with leather thongs. This gum is used in medicine ; it dissolves in spirits of wine.

We do not enter the village of Khalépa, the residence of most of the European consuls and of the wealthy merchants, but, leaving its gardens and vineyards on the right hand, pass below the walls of a curious fortified Venetian house, now used as a rough homestead, and continue to mount the broad expanse of scrub and heather which stretches upwards towards the frowning rocky masses of the Akrotiri.

From the first height above Khalépa a beautiful view of Canea, called Khānia by the natives, is obtained; the colouring of the landscape is exquisite : the waters of the wide bay, in the early morning intensely blue, become later in the day of a delicate sapphire or pale opal tint, and on this pure mirror the line of Venetian walls, built of the bright yellow earth of the country, encircles a cluster of white and pale amber-tinted houses, surmounted by many domes and snowy minarets. Beyond the city to the left, and at a short distance from the coast, the orange and olive groves and vineyards are dotted with sparkling villages, until the higher foliage ceases among the gorges and shrub-clothed uplands of the first line of hills ; towering above them rise the grand masses of the

CANEA FROM KHALÉPA.

To face p. 212.

'White Mountains' of Sphakia, clothed in snow during several months of the year; to the westward the view is bounded by the bold promontory of which Cape Spada is the north-western extremity, and in the pearly diaphanous haze of the northern horizon you trace the faint outline of Santorino and of other islands of the Archipelago.

We could not linger to admire this beautiful panorama; the way lay before us long and shadeless; the road itself, indeed, soon ceases and becomes a mere horse-track among shrubs and boulders of blue-gray rock. We are beginning to climb now in earnest; even the horse-track has ceased, and a faintly-trodden pathway among the heather leads round and often over the boulders. The Cyprian donkey is a tremendous animal, and well accustomed to this excursion; but the struggles at the sharp zigzag turns are terrific; my stout Cretan guide is forced to exert his utmost strength to aid the struggling animal; and so, scrambling, pushed, and encouraged, my very long-eared steed has gained at length the first plateau. The way is still utterly shadeless, but the mountain herb-scented breeze comes so refreshingly, and a grove of olive-trees in the distance has such a hospitable look, that we take fresh courage and trot on. The young Cretan, to enliven our progress, discourses on the marvels of the surrounding country. There are many ruined monasteries and chapels dotted about; their destruction dates from the Greek war in the early part of the century. One group of buildings, surrounded by trees at a short distance from the road, appeared in good repair and inhabited; it proved to be the chapel and holy spring of St. Anthony. Georghi says that many sick people go there, and after a short stay return to their homes cured; feeling, as I do at the moment, the pure health-laden breezes that are sweeping across the plateau, I think this result highly probable, but Georghi prefers to think it miraculous.

We are gradually nearing the cypresses and domes of the monastery of Aghia Triadha, on the second plateau, and in answer to some inquiries about the community, Georghi states that in former times this monastery was very rich, and that the reverend fathers were the terror of the country round, pillaging the unhappy peasantry, and committing all sorts of 'sheïtanlik' (devilry). Now, owing to some tax, which considerably lowers the pulses of the monastic revenues, they have become a quiet and respectable body. He says that the whole community is locked in at night. While I am wondering whether this may be a measure of precaution through fear of robbers from without, or of 'sheïtans' from within, Georghi hastens to explain that 'at the present time this is a good community of monks.' As they now number only twenty-three, they may still be called prosperous, in spite of taxation; they possess large tracts of olive-grounds and vineyards; they are very charitable to the poor, and in the season of the olive gathering employ sometimes as many as a hundred and twenty women to get in the harvest.

We have entered the shady groves of the monastery; for, as elsewhere remarked, the Cretan olive is a tree of great size, the heavy branches, laden with an abundant foliage, forming broad canopies of grateful shade. The near approach to Aghia Triadha is by an avenue of tall cypresses, a lofty flight of steps leading to the principal entrance. A black-robed monk, quickly observing our little cavalcade, comes forward to welcome us, and to lead the way through the strong gate in the fortified enclosure. The building appears to date from the time of the Venetians; it has been well kept up, and probably enlarged since then. Many cottages and outbuildings are scattered in the vineyards and gardens round about, but are only inhabited during the daytime; at night all retire to the shelter and security of the monastic fortress.

The chapel, a handsome building occupying the centre of the large quadrangle, is decorated interiorly in the usual style of Greek churches, with abundance of gilding and bright colours, Byzantine heads of saints, and a profusion of carving in wood, very beautifully executed, the work of a native artist. There are several smaller chapels, some forming part of the principal building, others detached. There was one to which the young Cretan guide, very anxious to 'do' the honours of the place, insisted on leading the way; it was a small domed building at the extreme angle of the enclosure—a bare, rough-looking room, with little in it except some planks and trestles, and a glass case fixed to the wall, containing two skulls, said to be those of the founders of the monastery; a door on one side was opened, showing a large dark closet very like a coal-hole; some pieces of board and an overturned barrow lay on the top of a high heap of what seemed like a fair provision of dry olive roots and sticks for winter firing; and while inwardly wondering that so small a detail of domestic management should be exhibited as one of the sights of the monastery, it was explained that we were gazing on the mortal remains of past generations of monastic fathers, taken up from an old burial-ground and thrown together in this irreverent manner, to await the construction of a fitting mortuary, which is, they say, commenced. I am inclined to think that the poor old bones will wait indefinitely.

It was a relief from the mouldy, unhallowed bone-house to pass back into the court, with the vine-garlands throwing their flickering shadows about the pilasters and galleries of the quadrangle. One wing of the building is prepared for the reception of guests, as it is very usual for families to come from the town during the hot season and to spend some time on this breezy plateau. The guest-rooms looked clean and inviting, the striped native coverlets and padded 'yorghans' all neatly folded and ready for use. In a pleasant room on the ground-floor the sweetmeats and coffee were politely offered by a deacon and by a serving 'brother'; the hegumenos was absent, and it appeared that some change in the government of the monastery was in contemplation.

The dress of these Cretan monks is much the same as that of the Greek priesthood elsewhere : a long black robe with wide sleeves, and a black, brimless hat ; their hair is long, sometimes streaming over the shoulders. Our guide over the monastery was a young man, tall, fair, and very slender ; he wore a faded lilac scarf, loosely wound about the waist of his rusty black stuff dress; his weak-looking, wavy curls and his slight figure, swaying like a reed, formed a curious contrast to the dark, strong, tight-looking little deacon, who wore his coarse thick plait of jetty hair snugly tucked out of the way under the black cloth cap. There was another member of the community, who came quietly in, with a tall wand in his right hand, a very little old man, who had been in the monastery longer than anyone could remember. He was so small that he seemed to hitch himself with difficulty on to the divan beside the deacon, where he sat silently staring at me, with twinkling, bright-blue eyes; his great age had probably emancipated him from the monastic costume, as he wore a short cloth jacket and a pair of monstrous black-leather boots.

All Greek religious establishments in this island are subject to the Patriarch of Constantinople, and the revenue accruing to the patriarchate must be considerable, as they reckon as many as thirty large monasteries in Crete, beside a great number of smaller religious communities.

Our entertainers were exceedingly hospitable, offering all the resources of the place—cooked fowls, mutton, wine (their wine is locally celebrated), or, in short, anything that could be named; but the opportunity for sketching was too precious to be wasted, and having brought some provisions, I made my way through the vineyard to the grateful shadow of a line of almond-trees, on the border of the olive plantation. The benevolent intentions of the good people were not, however, to be checked, and presently appeared an attendant neophyte, bearing a well-furnished tray — fried fish, cucumber salad, toasted bread, and an abundance of fruit, all very nicely arranged on clean white napkins. So my Italian attendant and Cretan Georghi sat down on their heels, sociably, with the deacon and one or two hangers-on, and regaled themselves, while the reed-like 'brother' wandered among the almond-trees, plucking the young fruit, and presently poured into my lap an offering of milky almonds; he had cracked them, I was thankful to observe, with a stone, and not with his teeth, according to a not unusual manner of native civility on similar occasions.

It was great 'kief,' resting in the cool shadow of those almond-trees, gazing on the quiet monastery, backed by the gray heathery mountain slopes, the utter silence only broken by the good-humoured voices of the feasters round the tray, by the tinkle of a distant goat's bell, or by the dry, creaking sound of a tall cypress swaying in the breeze. I could have gladly lingered here till sunset, but there was much more to see before our day's work could be accomplished, and especially the stalactite cavern, on the further slope of the mountain, to be explored. To reach this spot it was now made evident that yet another guide was needed; in these countries guides collect as you go on like rolling snowballs. He came forward after some delay, a jolly-looking, very sturdy peasant monk, bearing a huge key, and mounted on a stout mule; he looked equal to anything in the way of mountain climbing or cavern exploring; so, leaving with the deacon a present for the servants, we took leave of the good fathers of Aghia Triadha, and began once more the scrambling, stumbling progress among the boulders, crushing out sweet odours as the animals trod down the great lilac tufts of blossoming thyme and heather. The aromatic plants that clothe the surface of the Akrotiri are held in such esteem by the peasantry, that beehives from the villages of the plain are often brought here for change of food. A peculiar kind of sage grows in these parts, called by a French writer *sauge à pomme;* the natives drink an infusion of the leaves; it has a stronger scent and flavour than our sage tea, and is accredited with great medicinal virtue. My young Cretan at once stuck a large sprig of it behind his ear.

After winding up our difficult way for about half an hour, we enter a narrow cleft of the mountain between walls of rock, in some places scarcely a few yards apart, a wild cascade of boulders, with sharp turns at every few paces, till, emerging from the chasm, we gain a stony plateau, where, in the centre of a few meagre fields, stands the desolate-looking convent of St. John the Baptist. One patch of pale-green corn, and three stunted wind-blown trees, do little to relieve the forlorn aspect of the spot, the highest point of the promontory of Cape Melec.

Like all the convents here, as indeed generally throughout the East, St. John's is fortified by a crenelated wall, flanked by square towers at each corner, and with machicolated balconies as an additional means of defence. From the exterior nothing is visible above the wall but the summit of the dome of the chapel; the aspect of the place softens as you pass through the low arched gateway. A tiny garden and a dripping fountain enliven the approach to the chapel, and a very cordial old lady hobbles forward with a kindly welcome. She is the mother of one of the priests, and there are younger women (one of them very pretty), who gradually appear on the scene, offering quince jelly and coffee, which I take, seated in a homely little chamber on one side of the court.

The families of the married priests of the Greek Church usually dwell in the quadrangle, and in detached cottages in the gardens and vineyards; the monks, such as the community of Aghia Triadha, take the vow of celibacy.

It is difficult to understand why this place should be called a convent, for there was certainly nothing conventual about it. Six individuals seemed to represent all the human life of the establishment: the priest, a middle-aged man, newly come into this solitude; his wife, a gentle-looking pale woman, suffering from fever; the priest's old mother, too deaf to engage in verbal civilities, who nodded and smiled from a low stool in the corner of the room; the two young girls already mentioned, and a sort of peasant priestling hovering round about, made up the number of the community defended by the fortified walls of the monastery. The barren plateau had been enlivened a few days previously by a gay crowd of pilgrims gathered here to celebrate the festival of St. John; but the last stragglers had departed, and for another year an almost unbroken silence has fallen on the stony desert.

The church in the centre of the court is, like

most of the churches in the island, of Venetian origin; it was unfinished at the time of the conquest by the Turks in 1669, and has since remained in the same incomplete state; the columns intended for decoration had risen but a few feet from the pavement, and truly the loss of their upper proportions is not to be regretted, as it would be difficult to meet with anything in worse taste than the clumsily florid style of the sculptured bases; but the interior of the church is worth a visit, as the wood carving, extremely rich, delicate and correct both in design and execution, is due to a native of the village of Khalépa.

With a provision of tiny wax tapers we start once more upon our travels, having added to our company Guide No. 3, who conducts Guide No. 2, who shows the way to Guide No. 1, who is leading me; for now we leave the animals behind, as goats alone of four-footed creatures could be expected to master the difficulties of this track, a rugged defile leading towards the shore of the eastern slope of the Akrotiri. The jagged rocks, the boulders, and the aromatic herbs once more, but intensified, and requiring frequent pauses—for breath in the first instance, then for admiration, for it is most beautiful! On the left hand an almost perpendicular cascade of rocks and shrubs conceals the bottom of the ravine; the opposite rise of the mountain is softer; here and there a tiny enclosure and some faint traces of cultivation cluster round a rude hut of branches; or a dark hole in the mountain side, a desolate stony lair, marks the retreat of some extinct hermit; the faint tinkle of a goat's bell reaches us from the midst of the heather, and the black and white and gray and tawny spots are slowly dotting the stern surface of the picture. These are not the genuine wild goats of which the race is said still to linger amongst the White Mountains of Sphakia: they are a semi-civilized flock, and we come upon their home a few minutes later, as, turning abruptly to the right and down a steep plunge between a rude stone fence and the high granite crags, we are suddenly at the mouth of a dark cavern, and within sound of fresh human voices: two goatherds and the pretty girl from the convent above are joking and laughing over a great cauldron of fresh-drawn milk, as if life were a very gay affair in that desolate solitude. They are busy making curdled milk, but I rescue a glassful before the curdling has commenced, and pass on to examine the wonders of the place called the Cave of the Bear. A small rock-hewn chapel forms the entrance, which is sufficiently wide to give a view of nearly the whole extent of the cavern, a lofty, irregular rotunda, vaulted, and in part walled in with stalactites ; one great mass, partly rock and partly stalagmite, rises nearly in the centre ; it has a rough likeness to a huge bear, standing up and bending over a square tank of water, built in by a stone wall, said to be of great antiquity. The legend of the place avers that the unlucky beast, having come in veritable flesh and fur to slake his thirst at the ice-cold waters of the subterranean fountain, was then and there punished for his audacity, and turned to stone by the presiding saint of the little rock chapel. I took a sketch of the sinner, and, returning gladly to warmth and daylight, found the little group still busy with their curds and whey, the great cauldron simmering over a wood fire, built in a corner of the outer cavern, and presently (the curds having been ladled out and set to drain) it was borne away by

RUINS OF KATHÒLICO, AKROTIRI.

To face p. 216.

the stout youths to a hole in the ground, where the good sweet whey was thrown aside; then, with the merest apology for a rinse, the process of making curds was begun again upon a fresh quantity of milk. The method pursued is probably much the same all over the world, but the essential quality of cleanliness so dear to the true English dairymaid is held in small esteem by her Christian sisters in Eastern lands.

The sun beat fiercely on our heads as we stumbled down the rugged descent towards the last and most remarkable of the objects of the day's excursion, the ruined and abandoned convent and the vast stalactite cavern of Kathòlico.

The way was very precipitous, but presently a turn amongst the crags brought us in view of the sea, with the refreshment of the cool breezes sweeping up the narrow gorge; a staircase hewn in the face of the precipice leads downwards by one hundred and forty steps; from the middle of the ladder-like descent the remains of the great monastery may be seen, partly hidden in foliage and tangled creepers, far beneath in the gloomy ravine; a chapel here, a ruined archway there; strong buildings in decay; a broad bridge and archway spanning the awful chasm; on its rocky sides more cells of hermits among the wild vines and brambles, for the gorge, plunged in eternal shadow, is richly clothed with vegetation that relieves in some degree the utter desolation of this solemn, world-forgotten spot. It teems, alas! with bloody memories, for in the rock-hewn chapel of St. Elias, on the inner side of the ravine, twenty-four monks were murdered during the Greek War of Independence, and at all times the community, once numerous and important, were exposed to attack by brigands and pirates, who made their way up the gorge from the neighbouring sea-shore, till at length the monks of Kathòlico, greatly diminished in number, and dispirited, abandoned their weird solitude, and took refuge on the scarcely less desolate but yet less accessible desert plateau of St. John, on the summit of the mountain. In the stone pavement of the archway that spans the ravine a dark square hole is shown as the entrance to the prison for refractory brethren.

We prepare to enter the stalactite cavern, each one of the party holding a lighted taper. We follow our sturdy guide through a narrow passage and over vast masses of slippery stalagmite; then, squeezing with difficulty through a rocky cleft, come upon an open space, where it is possible to breathe and to admire the immense stalactites pendant from the roof; but the light of our feeble tapers is quite insufficient to produce the sparkling reflections which one expected. I can just discern that some of the columns are white and fresh-looking, while the greater number present a dirty gray or black surface. The heat is stifling; the slippery, rounded masses threaten at every step or scramble to shoulder you off into the inky pools of unknown depths from which they grimly emerge; the rushing of unseen cascades trembles through the still atmosphere, and the vast stalactites gleam, ghost-like and uncanny, through the shuddering darkness. The cavern winds on far into the heart of the mountain, but I decline to explore its utmost limits, and am contented to struggle to the spot, about halfway, where a great twisted stalactite, fallen down on the verge of a black watery hole, is (according to my guide) the punished form of a monstrous serpent, which had writhed itself there to drink at the uninviting source. The legend does not explain how the serpent should have existed there at all, unless he may have been of a *very* ancient race, as another legend declares that St. Paul, at the time of his visit to Crete, banished from the island all snakes, reptiles, wolves, jackals, and every sort of venomous and noxious creature.

Another legend relating to this same cavern I will give in the words of the narrator, Guide No. 2, as we had crossed the plateau of Aghia Triadha. 'The saints in these parts,' said he, 'are very powerful. I will tell you a curious thing that happened in the cavern of Kathòlico, which is, you know, a long hole in the earth—so long that no one has ever seen the end of it, and there are great dreadful pools of water, so that anyone that goes in without a light can never get out by himself. Well! there was the festival of St. Elias, and once a year all the people from the country round go to Kathòlico to pray in the little rock chapel of St. Elias, and some go into the cavern with one who knows the way, and with tapers. It happened long, long ago, that there was a poor man amongst the crowd who had no taper; he was very poor and weary and tired, and he went to sleep upon one of the great stones, and so he came to be forgotten, and was locked in. Well, see how wonderful this was: when the next year's festa came round again, some people as usual went into the cavern, and there they found this poor man still alive, but he was white—white—as white as snow, and thin like a skeleton, but still alive; and they brought him out to the air and light, and little by little his colour came back, and he got well.'

'And he had eaten nothing for a whole year?'

'Oh, nothing; there *was* nothing, but the saint had kept him alive, and he got quite strong again.'

On leaving the cavern for daylight and thyme-scented air, we bore away from near its mouth several beautiful fragments of spa and crystal; then, climbing the precipitous steps, we stopped to rest a moment at the Cave of the Bear; but the rest was very brief; the sinking sun gave warning to hasten our return to Canea, and, again, for the last time, we toil wearily upwards, merry voices echoing from the mountain side, as the girl and the goatherd come tripping along, bearing between them the heavy basket of cream-cheese, for the benefit of St. John's Convent.

Near the eastern angle of this building two

stunted olive-trees have grown into the most fantastic shape, from the great force of the wind rushing through the narrow cleft of the mountain.

The descent of the steepest part of the way was made on foot, our guide from Aghia Triadha leaving at the first plateau, and we heard the trot of his mule long after his good-humoured face had disappeared in the deep slanting shadows of the olive grove leading back to the monastery. We pushed on bravely, and, with rest and coffee at a little wayside establishment at the base of the mountain, finally reached Canea about an hour after sunset, very weary, but delighted with the day spent among the crags and gorges of the Akrotiri.

OUTER HARBOUR OF CANEA.

To face p. 232.

GHONIA.

It seems but yesterday, although a few years have flown by since that bright time, that, during a visit to the wife of Reouf Pasha, then Vali of Crete, the plan of an excursion towards the western shores of the island was arranged for us by this courteous and enlightened Governor, who promised an escort, a tent, and every possible facility for our little journey.

We were sitting in the large 'sala' of the konak, or Government House, overlooking on three sides the harbour, the blue expanse of the Mediterranean, and the distant headland of Cape Melec; through the open windows came the health-laden breezes of that exquisitely pure atmosphere, untainted by smoke of railway engine or factory chimney—breezes perfumed by countless aromatic plants that cover the wild stretch of common beyond the city. We could trace the roads bordered by aloes and cactus and blossoming bay and myrtle; the ravines, bright streams of rose-coloured oleander; and all the further spread of the plain—a dense mass of orange and olive and mulberry groves, the golden crosses of the monastery of Chrissopighi gleaming through the dark foliage at the foot of the Rhiza.

Crete, out of the line of modern travel, is seldom visited but by a passing yacht, or on the occasion of the anchoring of some ships of war in Suda Bay; then Canea wakens up, and festivities on board and on shore enliven the place; but these visitors seldom extend their excursions much beyond the city and its immediate environs, and have brought little or no change to the more distant parts of the island.

The preparations for our excursion had been rather elaborate, and the little cavalcade issuing in early morning through the western gate comprised, in attendance on Miss Y—— and myself, a captain of gendarmerie, two zaptiehs, two servants, and two baggage horses, with their 'suredjis,' one of the horses bearing the tent.

The way is a burning, shadeless track, as we wind along the moat of the Venetian fortifications, but the colouring of the picture is a great compensation: the massive bastion of reddish-yellow brickwork relieved against the softened green of a mound of aloes and prickly pear; beyond, a patch of yellow sand borders the intense blue of the Mediterranean; the pale lilac tone of the mountain range that ends in Cape Spada bounds the western horizon. We forget the burning heat, and soon the winding road takes us under the shade of a few trees, as we pass through the picturesque but melancholy leper village. Many victims of that hideous malady, most of them wrapped in great hooded cloaks, the hood drawn down, sit under the trees, or crouch by the wayside, begging, more as a semblance of occupation, in most cases, than from necessity, for a liberal allowance of bread is regularly made by the Government, and many of the lepers own property, the proceeds of which are brought by their friends and placed on a stone of the well that stands in the centre of the cluster of square whitewashed huts. A man on horseback, holding a little child in front of him, passes by; the child shows no appearance of the fearful taint that must inevitably declare itself as he grows older; but the hands that grasp the little plump, rosy form, have lost nearly all the fingers, and the featureless face of the unhappy father is almost hidden by the deep-shrouding cowl. The prevalence of this particular form of leprosy is attributed—in Crete—to the great quantity of salt fish and olive-oil consumed by the peasantry.

We have passed the leper village, and are crossing a well-cultivated plain, bounded always on the left hand by the beautiful foot-hills and the majestic snow-crests of the Sphakian mountains; we gradually approach a more wooded region, and at length, reaching the village of Alikianos, we feel stifled amongst the dense foliage of orange and olive groves. An orange grove in these parts—its poetical associations notwithstanding—is by no means, on nearer acquaintance, always the scene of enchantment dear to the poetic mind. On level ground it is dull, and unquestionably stuffy; nothing grows in the dark shadow of the heavy canopy of leaves, therefore the bare ground is varied only by the small ditches surrounding the black trunks for irrigation, and the whole is enclosed by an uninteresting stone wall. An orange garden on a mountain slope, as at Haròthia,

RUINED CHURCH ABOVE PERIVOGLIA.

To face p. 236.

where the trees drape the hillsides with a natural luxuriance of blossom and golden fruit, is charming to the stranger, though less productive, and therefore less satisfactory, to the owner of the beautiful wilderness.

An olive plantation in Crete is infinitely more picturesque than the orange enclosure; the trees here, dotted about the fields, grow to an enormous size, with shady, drooping boughs, and foliage of a much fresher tint of green than those of Southern France or Italy. Some trees sketched above Perivoglia, during another excursion, will give a slight idea of the majestic proportions of the Cretan olive.

As we wound along the airless and sultry lanes of Alikianos, we found that the caïmakam of the district, warned of the approach of the party, had ridden forward, followed by his secretary, to invite us to his fortified konak on the summit of the hill. It is a stiff climb, but we are repaid by the splendid view from the battlements of the surrounding country, and refreshed by lemonade and English biscuits. The whole of this part—frequently under water in the winter—is very feverish; two or three of the soldiers of the small garrison—although the castle is raised above the level of the marshes—were suffering unmistakably from this terrible scourge of ill-drained lands; but the conditions of existence seem to agree wonderfully with the orange-trees, which are, they say, the finest in this part of Crete.

Starting afresh—our cavalcade increased by the caïmakam, his secretary, and a few soldiers on foot—we followed for some distance the nearly dried-up bed of a torrent. It was intensely hot; the sun's rays, reflected from the sandy sides of the gully, and thrown up from the shingly bed of the watercourse, made the atmosphere almost unendurable, and it was a relief to find, as we descended the valley, that some streams of water must be crossed, giving an impression, if not an actuality, of freshness. One of these proving a little deeper than usual, a soldier jumped up behind Mario, the groom, who was riding; but the poor animal, already loaded with panniers, and thirsty, like all the rest of the party, stops in midstream, tries to drink, unsuccessfully, so he quietly subsides, flat, and rolls to get rid of his impeding burdens. We hear a shout, a splash, there is a confused struggling leap over the animal's head, Mario's blue cotton legs and the soldier's dingy cloth all in a tangle as they reach the shore, saluted by shouts of laughter and a declaration of no harm done.

We pass above Platània, once famous for its gigantic plane-trees, and here the caïmakam, having performed to the utmost limit the ceremonial escort of the parting guest, and exhausted all his compliments, takes a polite leave. We continue our hot progress for an hour or two, until a turn across a vineyard towards some spreading olive-trees brings us to shade and rest. We are on the outskirts of a small hamlet; it is decided to pass the night there, and the best cottage in the place—a new building—is hastily made ready. The room appears clean; there are finely-embroidered bed-curtains, and very handsome rugs of home manufacture, many-coloured, striped, and ornamented, hang from a beam suspended from the roof; but all this promising appearance is sadly belied by the undesirable presence of children, fowls, and a big dog, all difficult to expel, and by the immovable fact of a large heap of old rags, with some fleeces of uncleaned wool, lurking treacherously in a corner of that tempting-looking resting-place.

The next day, Sunday, was a weary time of waiting for our baggage-horses, which had gone on to another village, but they turned up at last, after ample leisure had been afforded for examining the groups of peasants sitting under the trees, with some slight improvement in dress, in deference to the day, but none whatever in the matter of cleanliness. It is a not uncommon prejudice with Eastern Christians to consider cleanliness as in some way an attribute of the Moslem, and therefore to be avoided by the Christian population.

Once more we are on our road to the monastery of Ghonia. It had gradually developed, as we approached, from a tiny white sparkle at the foot of the distant mountains to the appearance of an important cluster of buildings; but the light failed long before the end of the day's journey, and a great part of the way was a stumbling advance in the dark, chilled by heavy dews suggestive of fever and ague.

A most hospitable reception at the monastery soon consoled us for past tribulations; indeed, the worthy hegumenos, who superintended the arrangements, was overwhelming in his anxiety

WITHIN THE MONASTERY, GHONIA.

To face p. 240.

that we should be warmly covered. The night was sultry; the time midsummer. He had placed, first, a thick woollen quilt, doubled; then a large Sphakia blanket, also doubled, after which he inquired, with real solicitude, whether it might not be advisable to add a 'poplema,' or padded quilt!

In the morning, by mutual agreement, it was decided to give up the more extended scheme of travel, my friend Miss Y—— preferring to return to Canea, whilst I was to remain till the following day, to sketch some of the picturesque environs of the monastery, the captain of gendarmerie remaining also as my escort back to Canea.

The church and monastery of Ghonia are amongst the few that have escaped spoliation during the terrible struggles that have so frequently desolated this beautiful island; therefore, many of the pictures, although not beautiful, are old and curious; the profuse abundance of woodcarving is remarkably fine. The mountain rises abruptly behind the principal mass of buildings; the houses for the married priests, clinging to the steep slope, among orange and olive trees and great boulders of rock, are square, flat-roofed, gray stone dwellings, most effective subjects for the sketcher.

A little way up the hillside you reach the head of a small gully; immense flowering reeds are springing upwards from the bed of the unseen rivulet, and from this point the finest view of the wide sweep of the bay is gained, above the white domes and glittering crosses of the monastery. Canea, dimly seen in a blue and purple haze, appears to ride on the calm, azure-tinted sea.

Dinner in the room assigned to me would have been a quiet and solitary repast, but for the appearance of a witch-like, ancient dame, who hobbled in unbidden, sat on her heels beside the tray, and muttered what sounded like a long string of complaints, resolving itself into an earnest desire for backshish. The poor old creature—she was an evil-looking old lady—continued to wail and lament, until, pacified by the offer of a few copper coins, she finally consented to depart, and to leave me in peaceful enjoyment of the small, strongly-barred window that overlooked the terrace, with the soft lap of the tideless sea at its foot, and the shimmering band of silver moonlight stretching towards the vague horizon.

It is difficult to realize that this peaceful spot has been more than once the convenient landing-place for men and arms, sent to keep alive the disastrous warfare and struggles for which Crete has an unfortunate notoriety.

The Cretans have peculiar notions of the fitness of things, and of the uses to which English courage and enterprise may be turned for the benefit of their island. I was present one day when a certain vehement and hot-headed patriot endeavoured to enlighten our English Consul as to the special mission of England in the East. 'Why cannot your country,' said he, 'act with us as with the Ionian Islands: take Crete, put its affairs thoroughly in order, make it rich and prosperous, and then—simply hand it over to Greece?'

I left Ghonia on the following morning, attended by the captain, a careful and conscientious servant of the Pasha; a very picturesque young Cretan zaptieh, and Saïd, a negro, on the baggage-horse. We took, in returning to the city, the more direct road skirting the bay, which led over many a dry bed of a water-course, a mingling of shingle, oleanders in full bloom, aromatic shrubs, and tussocks of grass and heather. In a small village on the way peasants were lounging listlessly about with swarms of children, very idle. The captain tells me that Reouf Pasha has established schools in many places; has sent schoolmasters, and takes much personal fatigue and trouble in his anxiety to carry through this effort at improvement, but the people (unlike the Greeks of Attica, whose best quality is their eagerness for learning) will not send their children to profit by the opportunities offered. The captain is quite eloquent in praise of the Pasha and in blame of the idle peasantry, as we plod on and on through the sand, sprinkled with oleanders and an occasional olive-tree.

I am mounted on a pack saddle, raised upon a heap of rugs and felts, making a decidedly unsteady foundation, which is not greatly aided by a loop in a rope serving as stirrup; and there is nothing to speak of in the way of pommel, but the pace never quickens beyond a slow walk, so that the progress, while very fatiguing, is not dangerous, although the old gray horse shows an unfortunate tendency to stumble, and seems as glad as the rest of us when a halt is made under the rustic shelter of a roadside khan, which throws a few yards of shade across the burning sandy track. Here we rest awhile, refreshed by a glass of pure cool water from the little fountain; then on again, more sand, more dry beds of rills, until we reach a band of cultivation, and the large café of Platània.

An empty room on the upper floor has a rough balcony overlooking what the natives of Canea dignify with the name of cascades; it is a mill-race, the water rushing and foaming through three arches, amidst a wilderness of overhanging, leafy boughs; the floury miller is busily brushing out the room. I retreat to the balcony, shaded by thick vine-garlands, and enjoy, in delightful contrast with the glaring plain, what in the East is emphatically known as one form of 'kief'—rest in cool shade, beside running water. You must live in the East to appreciate the importance of water in an Eastern's conception of rural enjoyment; they will take you through a beautiful garden, such as that of Hamid Bay, near Canea; but the rich and glowing blossoms, the tropical plants and shrubs, are, to them, as nothing compared to the 'havouz'—a square tank of rather muddy water in front of a small pavilion.

Our horses needing the rest of an hour or two, and my captain also being glad of a long gossip with the master of the khan, I set off, followed by the young zaptieh, in search of the plane-trees, much vaunted by some writers, but they seemed to belong altogether to past history. A large fig-tree stretched its heavy arms invitingly in a good situation for the sketch of a village that climbs up and crowns a tall gray crag. Pashley calls this the site of the Cretan Pergamos; it is a cluster of square stone houses with flat roofs surmounting a fine sweep of olive-trees that drape the foot of the rock and spread across the landscape.

A Greek papass following his plough in a neighbouring field leaves his oxen to inquire what may be the point of interest to the stranger; he fails to understand, and I leave him, mystified, to go on my way through a narrow lane bordered by fields and orchards of mulberry, fig and walnut—the hedges are of aloes. Here and there I come upon a group of peasants in the leafy shade winding silk, the beautiful golden hanks hanging from the branches, the man doing the easier part, the winding, while the woman turns the heavy wheel. In many places there are cabins of boughs and flocks of snow-white sheep clothing the pleasant picture.

An ancient-looking Greek church on the summit of a high peak at a short distance seemed to invite inspection, but the way upwards between masses of rock, calcined by the burning sun's rays, looked appalling. We reached, however, the rocky platform of Platània, and from a yard or two of shade cast by a projecting crag, looked down upon the brown island of St. Theodorus, with its deep indentures or caves of intensely red earth, floating on a sea of liquid sapphire; the pale headland of Akrotiri bounding the horizon on the right hand. By a tortuous descent on the other side, a cascade of rocks serving as highway, we reach the fields, where, under the shade of some fine walnut-trees, I sketch the lovely scene, while my gay-looking attendant, the young zaptieh, enjoys an interesting conversation with a young maiden of Platània, who is drawing water at a shady fountain. The whole scene is so soft, so exquisitely beautiful in outline and colour, that it is difficult to turn from it and to regain the khan, the pack-saddle, and the sandy road; but one more short period of rest on the balcony above the gushing waterfall gave renewed energy for the last part of the little journey. The khandji's reckoning was more than moderate— for a luncheon of fried eggs, bread, cheese and coffee, served twice, and for the use of their best room and balcony for a great part of the day, I was asked to pay about fivepence.

The road now follows for a short while a pretty lane, which ends all too soon, and once more we are plodding along the open stretch of shore— sand, deep sand, varied by great stones and rocky boulders; but we are nearing home. The sand at length ceases, and we wind among the vast olive gardens below, two fortified villages gleaming white through the thick masses of foliage, the larger especially (Theriso) looking in the distance like a fortified palace standing in a magnificent park. We pass between the scarlet earth-cliff and the tchiftlik of Macri-teico (the Long Wall), and, turning eastwards, the Rhiza opens out to reveal the White Mountains, rising majestically with their snowy crests aflame in the rays of the sinking sun, and so, threading once more the way through the leper village, we pass the fortifications and alight in the court of the convent, which is our temporary home in Canea.

Before leaving the island I go to the enclosure of the military hospital, to sketch from thence the inner harbour and the ancient Venetian arsenal, with the noble range of lofty vaults built for the Venetian, galleys, now mostly in ruins; then, passing onwards to the Arab village, I quickly gather a wondering little crowd of black and brown children, with a sprinkling of men and women of almost every race to be met with in this corner of the Mediterranean. First, a tall Egyptian, having gazed wonderingly at my enigmatical manœuvring with book and pencil, appears suddenly enlightened, constitutes himself manager of the crowd, and suggests subjects. A wonderful old Arab, very tall, and entirely wrapped in a fearfully dirty blanket, is made to understand that he must remain quiet for a few minutes; he glares at the proceedings in a defiant manner, and when done, retires, stately. A passing Greek is pressed into the service; he is self-conscious, and twists his hands and legs into attitudes; then a negro with a water-jar comes on the scene; the attraction of a piece of money steadies him for a moment, while a handsomely-dressed Tunisian, advancing to see what the gathering means, declares vehemently that he *will not* be drawn, and I only catch the flow of his creamy bournous as he disappears amongst the wattled enclosures. There are a few negresses, and endless clamorous children; one mite, wrapped in some grown-up garment, with long hanging sleeves, presses to the front to stare with beady eyes through her ragged uncombed mane; a still smaller brown specimen ignores the proceedings, entirely absorbed in the possession of a rosy apple. All my subjects get coppers, till the purse is empty and I retire, still guarded as far as the highroad by the intelligent Egyptian, and followed by the group of youngsters, who had found the business of model lucrative, and strongly urge a renewal of the diversion.

AMONG THE HUTS, CANEA.
To face p. 250.

THE DANUBE AND THE BOSPHORUS.

THE DANUBE ROUTE: WESTWARDS, 1872.

IN connection with the recent imposing ceremony, the opening of the Iron Gates of the Danube, through which vessels may now pass with the speed and rush befitting the end of this nineteenth century, it may not be unwelcome to older travellers to recall the calm, leisurely, and rather torpid manner in which that famous passage —and, indeed, the whole journey westwards— was undertaken, and by many enjoyed, nearly a quarter of a century earlier, long before the present through system of railways existed in Eastern Europe.

After many years of unbroken residence in the East, I have started once more westwards to spend the summer months in the cooler climate of France and England. In these days of excursion tours and general wandering, the endeavour to relate one's adventures on such familiar tracks might look like an impertinent attempt to 'hold a farthing candle to the sun' of many another wider and better experience; but these experienced travellers are, almost without exception, such as come to our old-world countries full charged with their own notions of progress, and ready to judge everything according to their recognized standard; one can therefore venture to hope that there may be some attraction of novelty in the impressions of an old English dweller in the dreamy East going back into the midst of the eager, restless, hurried life of Western civilization.

And the Danube route through Europe, although so often followed, has been, until lately, rarely described either way.

I left Constantinople in the Austrian boat carrying the mails to Varna. It was in May, at which time of the year, with us, the weather is usually delightful; but we had already been suffering from intense heat and an unusual drought, so that the shores of the Bosphorus were prematurely taking their summer tint of russet and yellow, and the beautiful Judas-trees, which should have been still glowing with their wonderful blush of rosy blossom, had turned to ordinary masses of green leaves before their time.

We reached Varna early on the following morning; but the arrival at our destination did not imply that we were at rest. The calm, the peace, the gradual return to the interests of life, with a due solicitude for the care of our belongings, usual on such occasions, was not. We had arrived, and the rolling of the steamer, the pitching and tossing, were infinitely worse than before; for Varna has no harbour, and we were at anchor in an open roadstead in a rough sea. The preparations for landing; the descent into a crowded boat by the help of two sailors, who, watching the moment of its rise to the ladder, jumped you in all in a heap, before it sank into a hopeless abyss; the pouring rain under which I sat, utterly limp and helpless, till a compassionate neighbour, seeing me feebly grasping a closed umbrella, opened it, and placed it in my hand; the great swelling waves, tossing the boat up and down like an overladen nutshell—all these do not provide 'sunny memories' of travel by any means, and they are miseries which would have no existence if the project of a harbour, long in contemplation and so sorely needed for this much-frequented port, could be carried out in earnest. This system of embarkation in the dreaded Black Sea is positively dangerous for ladies and children when it takes place at night in stormy weather.

They were obliged to land us at a rickety wooden scala—the ordinary landing-place for the town—instead of at the jetty belonging to the railway, so that a further progress had to be endured on what, by a figure of speech, is called dry land; it proved to be a succession of mud-heaps and pools of water, through which the drenched passengers waded, in a very broken procession, to the train waiting to carry them on to Rustchuk.

Before we started many of my fellow-sufferers seemed to recover their spirits, even to the degree of laying in little stores of provisions for the journey ; it spoke well for the elasticity of their constitutions that they contemplated sandwiches favourably, and could even think with composure of a light refreshment of bread and country cheese ; for little else could be procured at the so-called refreshment-room, except weak greasy broth and weaker tea. A good Samaritan, a young traveller whom I had slightly known at home, made little excursions between the carriage and the buffet, bringing me these mild restoratives, and though I was still too ill to benefit by them, I felt the comfort of the kind care, and shall not easily forget it.

The neighbourhood of Varna is prettily wooded and undulating, with hedges surrounding the pasture-land and cornfields. The crops looked green and healthy, and did not appear to have suffered from the drought which, we heard, had almost ruined the vast tracts of corn on the further bank of the Danube. On the hill above Varna are several tumuli, similar to those near Kustenji on the plain of the Vardar, beyond Salonica, and in many other places ; they are said to have been left by the Goths, and subsequently used as beacons.

The railway runs for some distance between a long narrow lake and richly-wooded hills, with occasional patches of open cultivation, and here and there a sturdy-looking cluster of farm buildings or a little village. The rocky cliffs which for many miles overhang the valley on its eastern side are remarkable for their exact resemblance to ancient masonry, or fortified places with battlements and embrasures. There is the genuine ruin of a castle on one of the hills; but the illusion is carried on for an immense distance, and for picturesque effect is quite as satisfactory.

Many of the stations on the Varna and Rustchuk line are rural and pleasant-looking. We passed the Schumla Road station—reminding one of the Crimean War—and one or two others with strange names such as Shaitandjik (the Devil's Place), etc. As you approach the Danube the rocky hills and cliffs disappear, and for a time the country becomes rather flat. It is remarkable throughout for an agreeable absence of tunnels; you have the satisfaction of feeling as you pass along, at a not very alarming rate of speed, that you see pretty well all there is to be seen, and are well content to reach the mighty river at a point a short distance from the considerable town of Rustchuk.

This part of Turkey has a prosperous, cultivated look, testifying to the industry of the Bulgarians, the hardiest and most laborious of the Sultan's subjects. The railway must be of unspeakable advantage to the proprietors of the land, and yet, like all things new, in old-fashioned, out-of-the-way places, it has its bitter enemies, both biped and quadruped: the two-footed animals are fond of putting obstructions on the rails, and the buffaloes that occasionally take a fancy to wander about at their will are an obstacle no less dreaded and dangerous. Sometimes the sturdy patriarch of the herd, feeling perhaps his responsibility, will take upon himself to make a furious charge at the two fiery eyes staring at him with such unblinking intensity, and though his poor life is sacrificed, he probably succeeds in giving a dangerous check to the supposed enemy.

There is no sort of hotel at the Rustchuk station, which is at a considerable distance from the town, and tourists are here, as in many parts of the East, dependent on the hospitality of their countrymen. I found this most needful shelter and rest in the home of the director of the line, where, although I was unexpected, and personally a stranger, I was welcomed with most considerate kindness, and enabled to recover thoroughly before embarking on the longer, though infinitely less fatiguing, portion of the homeward journey.

It was pleasant to sit in the pretty morning-room, watching—beyond an acacia-shaded terrace —the lazy flow of the Danube, along which a black 'schlep' was heavily passing; or the bright little steamer running busily to Giurgevo with passengers for Bucharest, or, again, a large Austrian boat beating upstream from Galatz and Ibraïla, with sounds of gay music coming faintly across the water. On the opposite shore there is a long stretch of reeds and osier; further back, embosomed in trees, the roofs and spires of Giurgevo, bright and pretty enough at a distance. A railway now connects this place with Bucharest.

Rustchuk is fortified; but the town when you enter it has a mean, untidy look, and the inhabitants, in their everyday clothes, look more dirty than picturesque.

After a day's rest my kind host took me in his carriage to the landing-stage, where I hoped to meet on board my friend Mrs. W——, from Galatz, who was also going westwards. We had agreed to travel together, and as the *Szechényi* steamed into view from the reedy distance, I saw with great satisfaction my dear friend's kind face anxiously scanning the crowd that waited on the wooden 'scala' ready to embark.

We were travelling by what is called the 'slow service' instead of by the *accélérés* steamers, which at this season were sure to be crowded to excess. We had deck-cabins, and not being anxious to push forward at the utmost attainable speed, we were fairly comfortable, finding that the slow service has the advantage of showing you more of the life and manners of the countries through which it passes, as it stops at all the small stations along the river, taking up or setting down all sorts of passengers and goods.

The *Szechényi* was not at all crowded. I secured a delightful little deck-cabin; its windows, looking in two directions, might have commanded charming views, but for the slight drawback that there is absolutely *nothing* to be viewed. Anything more dreary and uninteresting than the northern or Wallachian shore of the Danube it is difficult to imagine : a flat mud-bank barely stemming in the yellow, sluggish-looking stream, yet just high enough to shut out any vista beyond it ; a scant covering of grass, which later in the season will be dry and indistinguishable from the muddy soil. At long intervals a Wallachian guard-hut, a small square block with a thatched roof and a high pole reared beside it, is the only object which for leagues and leagues stands against the sky, and breaks the horizontal line of mud-banks and water ; the thin grass, a few reeds, and the guard-hut, over and over again for nearly two days after leaving Rustchuk. The prospect was not teeming with interest. I was prepared for this, having already twice travelled by this same route ; but I knew that the Bulgarian shore is infinitely more varied, though not sufficiently fascinating to induce one to gaze at it through the windows of the great saloon, fast closed, and crowded with smokers, the deck being impossible from the heavy rain, for the water, so long desired, was now bursting in floods and waterspouts over a great part of Europe. Rustchuk, immediately after my visit there, was nearly half destroyed, and in

Hungary, Bohemia, and elsewhere, whole villages were swept away or inundated.

Our fellow-passengers were not of the class usually met with on the *accélérés* steamers, which are crowded with rich Russian and Wallachian families on their way to the German baths, with a sprinkling of Greeks from Constantinople, of English, and of tourists from everywhere. Our temporary neighbours were chiefly middle-class Moldavians and Wallachs, or, as they now prefer to style themselves, Roumàn; there were some Bulgarians also, and Servians, embarking for small distances, and taking only a saloon passage. In addition to this motley group, we were much interested in watching a very respectable party of Mussulmans, consisting of a 'cadi,' or judge, on his road to a new appointment at Semlin; some friends accompanied him, and the little party appeared to be in charge of an individual whose social status was not very clear; he looked like a Kurdish brigand chief, a powerful, swarthy man, wearing an aggressive turban, an enormous belt of formidable weapons, and gigantic boots; his voice was loud and strong, but his manners were softer than his aspect, and he was certainly inclined to look upon the surrounding 'ghiaours' in a conciliatory spirit. The cadi, a fine, grave-looking personage, very quiet and gentlemanly, was dressed in a loose cotton robe and furred pelisse, with wide cloth trousers, a broad shawl girdle, and a spotless white turban—the old-fashioned Turkish costume; one of his friends wore the green turban of a descendant of the Prophet, the others were not remarkable in any way.

A Wallachian family, occupying deck-cabins, were also going on with us for some distance. They were three in number: an old lady wearing an immense white hood, covered with a white veil, and showing on hands, arms and throat a vast abundance of jewellery; her husband, elderly, silent and unobtrusive; and a handsome sickly-looking nephew, who fortunately spoke French tolerably well, and, being very obliging, helped us to keep in check the charges for 'dàbls' (a supposed rendering of the idea of a 'table-d'hôte' dinner), and other hieroglyphical entries in the waiter's account. The rich aunt was on her way to Carlsbad; the nephew was going to Brussels to complete his studies.

The cadi and his fellow-Moslems, although perfectly sociable and friendly, did not eat with us: they had brought their provisions, and were served by their own people with caviare, hard cheese, yaourt, olives, and some very greasy hot dishes. The unusual life did not seem to agree with the poor cadi, for on the second day of our progress he lounged about very disconsolately, looked the colour of saffron, and was said to be suffering from a very bad headache. Towards evening we found him in solemn consultation with the old lady of the white hood; she was feeling his pulse, examining his tongue, shaking her head, and making desperate attempts to prescribe; but as neither party understood the other's language, it was rather difficult. However, Mussulmans have great faith in the medical knowledge of ancient dames in general, and the cadi submitted, being made to understand by signs that he was to imbibe a great part of the contents of an ominous-looking medicine bottle produced from amongst the treasures of the old lady's cabin; it did not seem to have effected a cure, however, for he looked the next morning just as yellow as before.

The tea and coffee on board these boats are

bad and very limited, but we were far too well experienced as travellers quite to rely upon chance in the all-important matter of tea. Mrs. W—— had wisely provided herself with an etna, spirits of wine, tea, sugar, biscuits, and a few other little luxuries, so we felt independent of waiters and badly boiled water, and having nothing enjoyable to look at abroad, consoled ourselves with afternoon teas, as prolonged as possible. Mrs. W——'s little daughter, a great pet of mine and a most delightful little companion on a journey, bright and gay, and gifted with a quick perception of the beautiful in Nature, made occasional sallies to report anything worthy of attention on the opposite shore; but there was nothing beyond now and then a distant village, a solitary farm, or a few men fishing on the Turkish side, while the weary Wallachian mud-bank continued unbroken; so we rested, and read a little, and looked at our watches a good deal, and discussed our fellow-passengers, wondered what the next steamer would be like (we were to change boats next day for the formidable passage of the Iron Gates), wondered what our friends were doing at home, wondered whether our cosy little party would float down the

Danube together again in the autumn, worked a little, found the weather intensely hot, and finally grew very sleepy, until roused by the preparations for dinner.

Such a state of semi-torpid existence would be intolerable if much prolonged, but for those (and it is a common case) who may be seeking change and rest after an overstrain of mind and body, the utter *far niente* is, for a day or two, decidedly beneficial. This river voyage is certainly the best method of beginning a journey; you have not to dread the suffering which, for many, renders a long sea passage almost impossible; you can expect no letters, consequently no disappointments, no visits, no news from the outer world, no excitement; you are in a sort of dormant grub state, gathering strength and energy before bursting into all the flutter and hurry and bustle of the life of cities, and the shrieking rush of railway locomotion.

The table-d'hôte dinners are good and well served. You have excellent soup of two kinds, the unfailing sturgeon, and a plentiful supply of preserved fruits to eat with the roast; tolerably good poultry, a variety of vegetables, a sweet dish, and a very liberal dessert of fresh and dried fruits. The charge is by no means excessive. I have the account by me, in which I find ' 1 dàbl 1 gulden 60 K.'; in paper-money, about three and a half francs.

In the course of the evening we passed Widin, and soon afterwards our course became for a short distance northerly. Our left-hand bank ceased to be Bulgaria, and we were skirting the Servian Principality. The boat stopped for a few hours during the night, starting again in the early morning. In due time I looked out. My cabin window faced the north. There was the interminable mud-bank just as before; on the Servian shore the same slightly hilly, rather pleasant country; but as the morning wore on shadowy blue forms of lofty mountains mingled in the far distance with the sky in front of us. Far away land-cliffs, with trees and hints of an occasional village, could be seen above the mud-banks, which in times of flood are often submerged, the water covering the whole flat country up to the base of these cliffs. Soon the Danube itself •became more animated. There were more schleps; a steamer passed; there were floats in the water, marking the nets laid down for the sturgeon; next we saw a black mill or two in the middle of the stream, and several men intently fishing; a few buffaloes gazed at us from the muddy bath in which they revelled; there was always the solitary guard-hut with its pole. But gradually the desolate horizon narrowed; the distant cliffs became more graceful; trees grouped themselves; we began to feel crowded! several schleps toiled slowly against the current; another busy steamer paddled hurriedly down the river; floats everywhere; more black mills busily at work. We aroused from our dreamy torpor to the animation of labouring, moving life. Signs of cultivation, fields, orchards, and cottages, were on either side. Our steamer wound its way carefully amongst a crowd of schleps and steamers and boats of all sorts, and we were thoroughly awake; for here was Turno-Severin, and the flat-bottomed boat was waiting to take us through the Iron Gates.

Before reaching the town, you remark two broken arches of very heavy masonry, the remains of Trajan's Bridge, and, within the limits of the place itself, a large enclosure of lofty trees is pointed out as a remnant of the primæval forest. Ruins of an imposing-looking Roman tower rise above the foliage.

Great quantities of sturgeon are taken at Turno-Severin ; it is said to be the finest in the river, and has been known to weigh as much as 100 okes (about 280 lb.).

We did not land here, but passed at once to the small boat which drew up alongside. The luggage was piled on the little deck, while the passengers bestowed themselves as best they might in the low-roofed cabin until the rain, happily abating, allowed us to take up our station at the prow, which is quite the best place for the full enjoyment of the magnificent scenery of a part of the Eastern Carpathians through which we were about to pass.

Our progress was at times very slow. The river boiled and foamed all around; a multitude of black, jagged, wicked-looking rocky points rose through the water on every side. It required the most careful and experienced steering to carry the little boat in safety through this intricate passage ; but the pilots thoroughly know their road, and I do not remember to have heard of a serious accident to any of the passenger steamers in this difficult part of the Danube. In the autumn, when the waters are much lower, the steamers are given up entirely between Turno-Severin and Orsova, and travellers are carried along the northern bank in carts and country vehicles of every degree of roughness; sometimes, also, these conveyances are used beyond Orsova for another portion of the river, which is full of eddies, though less difficult than the celebrated Iron Gates.

In ancient times the Romans, under Trajan, had constructed a road along the entire bank of the Danube. In places where the perpendicular wall of rock rises straight out of the water the road had been carried on upon great beams driven into the mountain, and overhanging the river, partly supported on an excavated ledge or shelf. The holes from which these beams projected may be clearly traced for a considerable distance on the face of the now inaccessible cliffs.

The scenery on either side of the pass is extremely grand : superb masses of gray crag, clothed with the richest and most varied foliage, which falls into a leafy wilderness in the clefts and dips of the summits, veiled and almost lost in the fleecy clouds that hurry wildly across the narrow glimpse of sky above. No sign of human habitation breaks the stillness of these primæval solitudes. An eagle swooping down a ravine, the shadow of a passing cloud, the leap of a fish, the thrill and wash of eddying water, increase instead of breaking the deep hush of nature ; and the impatient beat of our engine, the hum of conversation, the expression even of admiration, seem out of place and jarring on this solemn peace.

Sometimes a bend of the river showed more distant forest-covered peaks, blue and vaporous ; then, again, the giant wall of rock seemed almost to engulf us, with no vista beyond the crowning fringe of forest but the gleam of intense blue overhead.

At length the most formidable eddies were passed ; the passage widened on the approach to Orsova, although the town was still hidden by a sharp turn of the river, and it was before rounding this point of land that a little chapel, half hidden in a grove of dark cypresses, was shown as the spot where Kossuth had hidden for safety the iron crown of Hungary.

The air was sweet and heavy, with a scent as of immense hay-fields, long before we reached Orsova. It arose, we found, from great masses of a flowering wild shrub growing abundantly about this part of the shore.

Orsova, a frontier town of Hungary, stands in a mountainous and beautifully-wooded region on the northern bank of the Danube, which is narrow at this point. The opposite shore of Servia hems in the river with high mountains, clothed with wood to the water's edge. The little town itself recalls strongly one of the villages on the Moselle, with its clean little whitewashed houses, dark, overhanging roofs and simple church spire, relieved against the sombre mass of forest background. Orsova is the place of landing for the mineral baths of Méhadieh, better known as Hercules' Baths, at a short distance in the interior. These sulphur and iron springs have a widespread reputation, attracting many rich visitors, and the neighbourhood of Méhadieh, where there is a splendid hotel, makes Orsova, although in itself so humble, a very expensive place to stop at.

We landed at the Custom House, the luggage being carried by extremely black and coaly Hungarian porters. After a slight examination we followed our property to the nearest inn, understanding that passengers could not sleep on board, as the boats were to be again changed for the further voyage. They took us to a very ambitious-looking hotel opposite to the landing-place ; the master of the house possessed sufficient knowlege of bad French to let a room at an exorbitant charge, and as soon as the bargain was completed, it transpired that passengers were perfectly at liberty to pass the night in the larger boat that was going forward the next morning. We made the best of it, however, determined, if we had to pay for it, to profit by the rest in a genuine bed, and also to enjoy thoroughly the lovely scenery around Orsova.

It is a very bright and happy-looking little town, clean and cheerful, with a blaze of gay flowers in the shining windows of all the houses and cottages : fuchsias, roses, geraniums, etc. ; there seemed to be a general competition to display the finest blossoms and the brightest panes of glass ; many of the windows latticed, shaded by deep eaves, or half hidden behind a rustic colonnade.

Wandering along the quay towards the rural suburb, we passed two or three inns of small pretension, but clean-looking, old-fashioned and infinitely more attractive than our own temporary dwelling; it was either a White Horse, or a Golden Lamb, or a Crown, that charmed us by its whitewashed columns, latticed windows and brilliant flowers—a genuine gasthaus, not an imitation of a French hotel. Passing on through cool, dewy lanes, we came upon the highroad, shaded by tall lime-trees; there was a cross with its railing hidden in masses of the sweet-scented blossoms that had welcomed our approach to Orsova; the sun, setting in a soft golden haze, lighted up the beautiful wooded heights on the Servian shore of the Danube; peasant girls and children were bringing water from a roadside fountain; sleek cows wandered slowly homewards; Wallachian women passed us and stared, and we gazed at them in return, for the dress is one of the most picturesque that can be seen. They wear the long garment of coarse linen with wide sleeves which is so general in many parts of

Europe where women, working much in the fields, need the free and unencumbered use of their limbs; over this a coarse sleeveless jacket, then a very wide belt richly embroidered with spangles and colours; below this, again, a broad flat band, open at the sides, and also richly ornamented, from which hangs a heavy woollen fringe a full yard in depth, a sort of double apron of fringe, which waves and flows in the most graceful manner with every movement of the wearer; it is usually red, though sometimes of mingled threads, according to the colours used in the embroidery of the belt. These women wear their hair in heavy braids with a small brightly-coloured handkerchief, bound by a narrow plait of hair crossing the forehead.

The costume of the men consists of coarse linen shirts, ornamented with a rude kind of open work, dark sleeveless jackets, broad leather belts and loose linen trousers, also embroidered round the ankle; black pork-pie hats, with a little feather on one side, and half-high leather boots complete the everyday dress; they are a little more ornamented for holiday occasions.

Several peasants came on board; they had

intelligent, honest-looking faces ; some others also embarked from small country stations wearing enormous hats and heavy sheep-skin cloaks— Sclavonians of the ancient military frontier which formerly extended from the Carpathians on the east to Croatia on the north-western limits of Turkish rule. The inhabitants of this important tract of country were bound to hold themselves ready on all occasions to rush to arms in defence of Christendom against their aggressive Moslem neighbours, and they were endowed in return for this half-warlike state of existence with certain privileges and immunities, and were governed by exceptional laws. Much of this has been abolished, as the need of such armed watchfulness ceased, but the rugged-looking inhabitants have certainly made little change in the outward man for many centuries past.

The early sunbeams gilded the beautifully-wooded summits on either side as we left Orsova, but our departure was not accomplished without a heavy tribute to the rapacity of our host, strongly favoured by our unfortunate ignorance of Hungarian or even of German ; so he dashed the florins and kreutzers into the little account with an unchecked freedom, all the more trying that we were perfectly aware of the imposture; it had twinkled in his eye from the first, but resistance in French would have only produced an overwhelming flood of gutturals. The steamer was whistling frantically; there was no remedy but the mild recourse of determining never again to favour him with our society, and we departed, soon forgetting our grievance amidst the glorious scenery around.

The new steamer was larger than the one that had carried us through the Iron Gates, though of very light draught, as there were still some hours of difficult steering in the shallow, eddying water. The weather was delightful, as if to compensate in the most interesting part of the river for the tedium of much of the previous voyage. The mountains on either side after leaving Orsova are beautifully clothed with every variety of forest tree. On the northern bank you find again in many places the traces of Trājan's road carried along towering walls of gray rock rising perpendicularly out of the river. The unbroken sublimity of these massive forms, with no intervening gradation to give the eye the measure of size and distance, produced for a moment a singular illusion. Looking steadily across the smooth stretch of water upon a stupendous mass of granite, I thought I saw a tiny object floating at its base like a child's rough toy-boat; and while I wondered how such a thing could be found so far from human habitation, a slight movement on the little toy showed a minute gray object, which for one bewildered moment I could imagine to be a very small monkey. Of course it was an ordinary fishing-boat with a full-grown fisherman looking after his floats near the edge of the stream, but it was really difficult to force the eye and brain, filled with the grandeur of stupendous forms, to a true comprehension of the relative size of smaller objects.

The Danube was exceedingly shallow in many parts of the morning's progress, requiring three or four men at the wheel, and a very slow and careful advance. There are times and seasons when the water is sufficiently high to enable the large boats to perform the whole journey without change; at others the navigation becomes altogether impossible, and the vehicles already mentioned must be used.

On the northern bank the modern road runs along with little difficulty, as the land on that shore rises more gradually, even breaking away into lovely valleys with meadows and patches of park-like cultivation. For three hours the scenery was beautiful beyond description, the wilder grandeur being on the Servian side of the river, whilst among the softer beauties of the opposite side little hamlets nestled in orchards and leafy copses; then a kind of Robinson Crusoe hut appeared perched in an old tree-stump; peasants tossed the scented hay; the broad leaves of the Indian corn swayed with the breeze, and above all this the stately forest-clothed summits rising into the clouds and broken by masses of gray rock lowered sometimes their sombre crests to give shadowy glimpses of more distant mountain peaks. One mountain on the northern bank rises from an ocean of foliage, a giant cone of naked granite. It was near this point that we passed a coal-mine in full work, and it is about this part of the Danube that the lofty mountain wall shows a remarkable geological formation, thrown up as it were in gigantic billows and surging waves of many-coloured strata. The effect is solemn and imposing in the highest degree, and forms perhaps one of the most interesting features of the scenery of this noble river.

At Drenco, or Drencova, we again change boats, embarking on the fine steamer the *Ferdinand Maximilian*. The character of the country has changed considerably, but is still very attractive, as the river winds about small islands and sharp points of land. At one moment you see a town quite ahead; we are apparently drawing near to a landing-place. Not at all! The boat gives a sharp turn, and the town is on your right hand, then on your left; finally, we do not approach it, and the passengers for that destination are landed on a rough pontoon near a wild stretch of pasture-land, and you see them mount into the carts, cabriolets or char-a-bancs, waiting on the bank, and go gingling away towards the spires and sparkling roofs that gleam far off through a tangle of waving trees. Sometimes, however, the towns stand by the river bank, and we run close up to them. At one place in Servia, evidently an important station, a sheep and cattle fair was in preparation. Great numbers of rude covered carts wound slowly up and down a steep hill above the landing-place; all the open space for a great distance was crowded with flocks and herds, and some hundreds of Servian and Bulgarian peasants; men, women and children, picturesque and very dirty, gazed at us as we gazed at them, and were mutually gratified, as nearer acquaintance with those 'great unwashed' would not have been desirable.

There is somewhere about this part of the Danube a lofty peak of gray rock rising abruptly out of the river; it has some curious legend attached to it, which, unhappily, we failed to learn.

In the course of the afternoon we passed Semendria, with its grand, irregular, many-towered old fortress, standing boldly out into the river on a commanding headland; two flags were waving on the principal tower on the side towards the town: the Servian, large, bright and flaunting, while the poor little faded Turkish ensign flapped meekly beside it, quite overpowered and subdued by its vigorous-looking neighbour. A ruined Mussulman tomb, almost hidden in a sombre grove near the fortress, and beyond this a great natural amphitheatre of sandstone cliff, covered with trees along the summit, irresistibly recalls one of the most fearful incidents in the barbarous warfare which for centuries ravaged and desolated this part of Europe; for it was in such a spot as this that one of the Sultans came suddenly upon a spectacle almost without parallel even in the frightful annals of that bloody period—thirty thousand men, women and children impaled by the Wallachian Vlad (justly named the Devil), in order to strike terror into the heart of his Moslem conqueror.

Not far above Semendria the boat stopped at Basiasch, the first point in the grand network of Austrian railways, and here several passengers left us, preferring to continue the journey by train. If speed, however, is not the first consideration, it is far pleasanter to remain on the river, at least, as far as Pesth; it is less fatiguing, and the railway line passes across a flat, open country, hot, dusty, and uninteresting. We remained on board, and it was quite dark when the steamer, turning up the Save, stopped at Belgrade, disembarked some passengers in the pouring rain, and then returned across the Danube to Semlin for the night. In the early morning we steamed once more to Belgrade, to take in other travellers.

The aspect of this celebrated city was rather disappointing; the fortress, it is true, standing on a bold promontory, is a striking and picturesque object in the foreground, but the rest of the picture is wanting in effect—pleasant and nicely wooded enough, but not sufficiently undulated for beauty.

Leaving the Save, once more we pursue our course, which at first is northerly, then turns westwards, until, beyond Peterwardein, it runs straight up due north as far as, and even beyond, Buda-Pesth.

The left-hand bank of the Danube continued fertile and pleasant, and the opposite shore again, for a few hours, flat and monotonous; but gradually a more populous part of the country is reached— towns, villages, and hamlets increase in number. We stop at several stations, amongst which Carlovitz, with its vast monastery and commanding situation, makes a very fine effect.

We are now in Hungary, and as the frequent stoppages brought a continual variety and change amongst the passengers, we had full opportunity of admiring the tall, slight, elegant figures of many of the Hungarian ladies; their easy, graceful carriage, and the delicate, refined cast of head and features ; but these charming women should be seen in gloves, as their hands by no means correspond to the elegance of the rest of the person. They are good useful hands, which, to their honour be it said, are capable of, and accustomed to, performing all kinds of housewifely work, but yet, might they not contrive to preserve a little more of the softness and charm which Nature must surely have bestowed upon them ?

Two very pretty Hungarian girls came on for a short distance from one of the country stations ; the elder patiently and very fruitlessly endeavoured to enlighten my inquiring mind on some questions of national costume by alternate efforts in Servian and Magyar speech. It was useless, and I was fain to content myself with thinking how pretty she looked, with her clear skin, rich chestnut hair, and soft, earnest brown eyes, and afterwards (there was nothing of interest on either shore just then) I fell to taking mental notes and measurements of two of the most wonderful, preposterous, and exaggerated chignons which it had ever been my fate to encounter. The unfortunate wearers, who had lighted up with all this blaze of fashion our sober-looking group of passengers, came from little country stations. They held different views on the subject of adornment : there was the stern and massive style, and the fuzzy, frizzy, bewildered, uncombed work of art— this unkempt structure reached by careful mental measurement a face and a half above the forehead of the lady. The severer style of hair architecture consisted of monstrous braids of black hair, so massive, so ponderous, that they seemed to overpower the thin neck and wrinkled face upon which they were heaped, obliging this victim of 'fashion' to sit bolt upright for long hours ; to recline, or to make any hasty movement, would have imperilled the whole fabric.

Other ladies around us, more sensibly attired, were provided with work or books ; for the scenery here was not varied, the principal feature of the river being floating mills, black, lumbering objects, with the name of the owner in large letters on the side ; some were heavily at work ; some motionless. We passed them at intervals throughout the day, ten or twelve in a group.

Approaching Buda-Pesth, the Danube is covered with a labyrinth of uninhabited islets ; we wound about them in the most puzzling manner, seeming to be running in every direction except the right one. Nothing can be conceived more intensely mournful, dark and dreary, than these islets— dense plantations of poplar or willow; on some, trailing wild vines break the intolerable uniformity of the sombre outline; more often they rise from the water, a serried mass of heavy foliage, supported by perfectly upright meagre tree-trunks, that look bare and pale and ghastly against the impenetrable gloom beyond. The only objects to vary this depressing stretch of river scenery are the black mills again, and again, and again. We were heartily glad when desolate jungles and black mills became alike indistinct in the gloom of night, and the steamer anchored for awhile at Mohatch.

Matters had decidedly improved the next morning. We had made some progress, and now villages, cottages, habitations seemed to pass along in a moving panorama on either side of the Danube. We landed or took in passengers all day, until late in the afternoon we reached the termination of our long river voyage, and landed on the quay at Pesth.

We went at once to the Grand Hôtel Hungaria, a really beautiful building, which has arisen together with a whole row of splendid mansions on the new quay, where exactly ten years previously I had seen merely open ground between the river and the city; but, as everyone knows, Hungary has since that time gained a great political triumph in crowning her King in the capital of her ancient and warlike country; and the new buildings, the animated streets, the prosperous-looking shops, the stirring life into which the traveller is so suddenly plunged from out the dreamy existence of the river journey—novel and bewildering though it may be at first—make a strong impression of the healthy impetus given to energy and progress; for pictorial purposes, however, I liked the place better in the former time.

The Hôtel Hungaria is furnished with all appliances of the highest civilization: electric bells, speaking-tubes, tiny boy waiters in dress-coats and white ties. It seemed very strange at first, the constant roll of vehicles—to us an almost forgotten sound — the brightly-lighted, central glazed court, the glittering supper tables, the flowers and shrubs, the gay, bustling scene. It appeared to wipe out, for the moment, years of our quiet Eastern life. As our rooms looked into this court, it was amusing to watch for awhile the different groups of feasters, both ladies and gentlemen; the busy waiters and pompous little boys, hurrying about in all directions, balancing three or four different dishes on their arms, popping corks, taking orders, or insinuating advice to some forlorn foreigner lost in the hopeless mazes of a German *carte*. It was like looking down upon a pantomime; but one evening's entertainment is quite sufficient; the glare, the noise, with the heavy vapours of rich sauces with which the heated air is charged, were sickening and oppressive.

A few hours of rather desultory rambling the next morning showed many changes and improvements both in Pesth and in Buda. In front of the suspension bridge may be remarked a small mound; four short paths, bordered by stone parapets, lead to the summit, which is, indeed, raised but slightly above the level of the roadway. This is the artificial mound composed of earth taken from all the different parts or counties of the kingdom, and it was here that the Emperor of Austria went through the final ceremony of his coronation as King of Hungary. He had received the iron crown and the ancient mantle of St. Stephen in the church of Buda, and, crossing the suspension bridge wearing these royal emblems, took certain oaths of fidelity as the guardian of Magyar liberty before the townhall. After this ceremony, he urged his somewhat restive charger up the coronation mound, turning him, whilst he waved the sword, successively towards the four points of the compass.

Wandering in a labyrinth of winding streets, between handsome houses and brilliant shops, we enjoyed thoroughly the unaccustomed pleasure of walking on flagged foot-pavement, and of admiring the sturdy dray-horses, with their fine harness ornamented with plates of brass scrupulously burnished; many parts of this harness are as light and elegant as those used for English carriage-horses. On the occasion of my former visit to Pesth the appearance of these handsome drays had made a great impression. At that time, also, the Hungarian national costume was almost universal. The man who served you from behind the counter wore top-boots, ornamented tights, a braided buttonless jacket, and a long beard, looking like a nobleman in reduced circumstances. Now the national dress seems almost to have disappeared, as all characteristic costume disappears everywhere before the all-levelling scythe of railways. The more's the pity!

You cross the suspension bridge to enter Buda, a large and busy-looking town, more picturesque than Pesth on account of its fortress-crowned hill, the Blocksberg. On the summit of that hill, and from a terrace near the ancient church, a most beautiful view is gained of the twin cities and of the Danube winding away towards Vienna through a tangle of wooded islets. On the left hand, among fields and vineyards, you see a solitary Mussulman tomb, much venerated and visited by such of the faithful as pass this way. A special clause in the treaty of peace between Turks and Christians, signed at Carlovitz, provides for the security of this Ottoman shrine.

The ascent on foot of the Blocksberg is very fatiguing, although it has been made as pleasant as possible by paths plentifully furnished with seats; they wind in zigzag upwards through a shrubbery. There is, however, a wire-rope railway up the perpendicular face of the cliff, starting from the left of the entrance to the tunnel; for this picturesque hill appears to have occupied public attention a good deal of late years. A magnificent tunnel has been pierced through its very heart to connect the city of Pesth by the bridge with the country on the further side of the mountain. The tunnel is a splendid specimen of solid and highly-finished work.

Owing to a delay occasioned by a missing travelling trunk, I was obliged to remain behind, when my friend Mrs. W——, with her little daughter, took their places in the train for Vienna. The little episode of a frantic, and for some time unavailing, search after my vagrant property remains only vividly in my memory; and no less vividly, and most gratefully also, the recollection of the exceeding kindness shown by a Hungarian gentleman, a perfect stranger, who, seeing my perplexity, devoted himself for more than an hour to the search, and finally unearthed it in a distant goods depôt, standing on its head, and looking utterly forlorn, disreputable, and cast away.

I started by the night express, and reached

Vienna in the morning in a pitiless downpour of rain.

A noticeable feature among the changes that have taken place since my first visit to Vienna is the filling up of the moat. Ten years ago they were just beginning to build there, and many large spaces of garden and meadow still isolated a good part of the old city from the suburbs. The new Ring Strasse, bordered with magnificent groups of monumental buildings, is certainly very fine; yet, one cannot but think that the health of the city, and undoubtedly its characteristic feature and picturesque effect, have equally lost by the 'improvement.'

We started for Cologne by Lintz, Passau, and the Rhine. The rain had cleared off in a pleasant glow of evening sunshine, and the lovely environs of Vienna could be thoroughly enjoyed. Hills richly wooded; charming villas surrounded by their parks and gardens; cottages beside little streamlets seen through shady boughs; the leafy trees, heavy with the moisture of the late rain, showering diamonds as the soft breeze swept across them; the rich green corn, not beaten down, but refreshed, and rejoicing once more in the ripening rays; solemn cows slowly winding along the thick pastures. Then all is suddenly lost in a deep cutting; a rush through yellow sandstone, which ends as suddenly, and you are passing Mölk, the superb Benedictine monastery, gloriously crowning a vast rock that rises abruptly above the river; and in the same picture, at the next turn of the river, and on its bank, the old castle of Durnstein, where some say that Blondell sang to the imprisoned king; the glistening Danube, the soft pastures, the wooded heights, the nestling villages again. Another rush through the sandstone, a sharp turn in the line, and once more a bright opening, through which, for one eager moment, you see Mölk again; and while striving to decide which picture pleases most you are engulfed in a tunnel. When you next see daylight the noble monastery and the ancient castle are left far behind, and you are whirling past white and brown thatched cottages, past rustic little chalet-like stations covered with creeping roses, and shaded by acacias in full bloom. Sometimes a ruined castle on a rocky cliff or lofty hilltop breaks the softer outline of green woodland, or a rustic bridge in the valley beneath blends with the gray shadows creeping gently up the landscape; and so evening wears into night, blending all in a mysterious dreamy uncertainty, from out of which tiny sparks wink and blink, sometimes in a cluster, sometimes a solitary flash, till at length you rush into a lighted busy station—Passau— and arouse to the necessity of movement; for here the baggage must be examined, and the train changed on to another line of rail.

Passau, of which in this manner you have not the slightest glimpse, is well worthy of a daylight visit, for its beautiful situation, its curious churches and votive chapels, and for the remarkable point where the three rivers—the Danube, the Inn, and the Ilz—meet. The Danube flows a muddy yellow; the Inn is clear and brown, while the Ilz looks like troubled milk. The three streams run together for some distance, without entirely mingling their waters; the Danube, as the nobler river, seems to pursue its course regardless of the little tributaries tumbling about each other and curdling like thick cream in a flood of strong tea.

We have entered Bavaria, and continue to rush westwards, passing Ratisbon also in the night. It is almost a pity to take the rail along this route from

Vienna; seen from the river, the whole distance thus far is wonderfully beautiful and interesting—infinitely preferable (as the guide-books declare) to the most vaunted scenery of the Rhine; but the accommodation on board the little steamers, which alone are able to make their way along the upper part of the Danube, is so extremely bad, that it requires a very deep love of the beautiful to induce travellers to take that route in preference to the easier journey by rail.

Ratisbon is still more interesting to visit than Passau. The magnificent cathedral, the old Rathhaus and torture chamber, and that wonderful piece of antiquity, the Scotch church, with the curiously carved porch, and the quiet cloisters where many a noble Scottish name is cut on the funeral slabs of the time-worn pavement, are well worthy of a slower progress through this beautiful and interesting part of Central Europe. The only satisfaction, however, to the curiosity of the hurried railway traveller is—a station and a name!—so, submitting to the inevitable, we rested in the comfortable railway carriage, to awake the following morning surrounded by the wild and varied scenery of Bavaria. It is a rich mixture of wooded heights, with gray crags rearing their crests above the surging masses of green; then we pass Amberg, a quaint old place, with its ancient castle and moat, its turreted gateways and majestic avenue, and immediately afterwards Sulzbach, wonderfully picturesque, a vast antique building on a rocky cliff, with the little town clustered about its base.

The scenery softens once more. Ever and again we shoot past hop-fields crowded with peasants busily dressing the poles; past meadow and vineyard and corn-field; past Nuremberg, and then the neighbourhood of Kissengen, about which part the aspect of the country becomes rather less attractive; and, fatigue overcoming curiosity, we decide to break our journey at Wurtzburg, where, about the middle of the day, we arrive at the clean and comfortable Hôtel de Russie.

We have now quite forsaken our old friend the Danube, on or near which we have been travelling for so many days, and our interest is transferred to the river Maine, which flows through the many-spired city.

We made very pleasant acquaintance next

morning with this river, winding through peaceful, smiling valleys dotted with hamlets and homesteads, reflecting in slight ripples the modest village, the delicately tapering church spire, or the solid barge drifting lazily upon its current. Occasionally a ruined castle on a distant hill, a forest-crowned height, a country residence with park and gardens, gave strength to the background of the quiet picture, an infinitely soothing sort of panorama for tired travellers to gaze upon, not requiring the exertion of ecstatic admiration, needing only a murmur of gentle satisfaction from time to time, passing gradually into a dreamy appreciation of things in general, and so on and on. . . . We are suddenly startled into life, rushing with a deafening clatter along an imposing structure—half bridge, half fortress—over a broad span of island and water; massive red towers rise on either side. What is this? Where are we? More red towers on the further shore reveal an old friend, Mayence, and we are crossing the Rhine. A pause in a sooty terminus; a whistle and a shriek, and we are speeding on our way towards Cologne.

What can I venture to remark about the Rhine,

the much-enduring, half-Anglicized Rhine? Does not every tourist with a ten-days' holiday know beforehand everything about it? Has not all its freshness and novelty been long since worn away by circular excursion tickets and cheap railway fares?

Alas, poor Rhine! I had seen it first in its unsullied beauty, when the sweet breeze swept over it, fresh and pure, with no more smoke curling about its orchards and its terraced vineyards than the light vapour from the cottage chimney, or from the charcoal-burners' encampment in the forest clearing. There were busy, crowded, toiling cities then as now, with chimneys that knew what real smoke meant; but cities have their limits, and cannot soil and blacken more than a given surface of earth's garden ground. Now—— well, it is needless to say more: the day was very gray and dull, making matters worse, and causing the dirty smoke of the shrieking engine to seem heavier than it need have been. The railway list of stations also, raising visions of sweet spots treasured in the gilded storehouse of youthful memories, was a bitter delusion and a snare. You see nothing of quaint, old-fashioned Bacharach but a dirty station, and, for one momentary glimpse, the exquisite tracery of St. Werner's ruined chapel. Oberwesel is uncomfortable ; it is impossible to find the right point, and the striking objects which, seen from the level of the river, form such a perfect combination of varied beauties, are now, as the line twists about like an uneasy serpent, everywhere at once, and all in a tangle together. We look down upon the roofs of sweet St. Goar, instead of upwards to the beautiful heights which overhang it ; and what has become of the famous echo of the Lurlei ?—that overworked Siren must surely at last have become so bewildered between trumpet-calls and railway whistles that she has given up the business in disgust. Where, also, are many of the famous ruins? They are above, behind, on one side or the other, and you see little or nothing of them. Ehrenbreitstein looks positively mean, seen too much on a level ; in short, a railway rush along the Rhine only creates vexation of spirit, and you feel that you have principally observed coaly stations, crowds of very ordinary tourists, and a great many advertisements concerning ale and bottled stout.

We are nearing Cologne ; the monster crane which was such a prominent feature of the Cathedral, a landmark for miles away, has for many years given place to the completed towers ; so, that is well! and doubtless that splendid bridge connecting the city with Deitz is also very fine ; I must strive to wipe out of my remembrance the picturesque old bridge of boats, with its wooden railing, on which the lounging Prussian soldier leant and smoked solemn pipes, while the spike of his helmet glittered in the sunbeam ; and the country women, with yet some remains of national costume — especially about the head— crossed and recrossed, carrying their marketings in large, useful covered baskets.

Cologne is greatly enlarged and improved, but Jean Marie Farina—several of them, and each one the genuine individual—is unchanged ; railway communication, by encouraging, has perhaps increased the number of the unit ; otherwise Jean Marie Farina is more Cologne than Cologne itself.

I was bound for Paris, towards which place I was taking rather a circuitous route, in order to enjoy as long as possible the loving companionship that had brightened the journey hitherto. But the moment came at last; we parted at Verviers, and I went on my solitary road sadly missing my kind friend and her sweet, bright little daughter.

Everyone now knows the banks of the Meuse, which rise into grandeur about Namur and Huy: the beautiful mixture of rock and forest on the one side, and the clear river on the other: the occasional tall chimneys that tell of mineral wealth and busy toil, and the rich cultivation of the open fields. The situation of Huy, although the glimpse obtained is too distant and too rapid, is beautiful, grouping together the river, the bridge, the old Cathedral and the crowning fortress on the lofty rock.

After passing Charleroi, pictorial effect and sentiment give place to coal, with a struggle at first between the wooded heights, the waving corn and scented hayfields, and the grim reality of factory chimneys; but at last the chimneys get the best of it, and reign supreme amidst soot and cinders, striving, however, to console you with evidence of the industry and wealth of all this toiling region.

It was at the buffet of the French frontier town that—almost for the first time since leaving Constantinople—I enjoyed the perfect satisfaction of complete and unclouded comprehension of the change received for my money. Ever since the moment of departure from the land of piastres, small change had been a tiny thorn in the path of our well-ordered progress, pricking its little difficulties from time to time, until it reached a climax, after passing Vienna, with complicated calculations between paper money and 'silber groschen,' and spread into an inextricable maze in the rapidly shifting German States. It was humiliating in the extreme to feel one's self obliged, for a very trifling payment, to place a silver piece before the waiter, and tell him to help himself; the loss to the purse was small enough after all, but the injury to one's dignity and self-esteem was not to be trifled with, and the making-up afterwards of accounts was accomplished with a bold freedom in the right hand columns which it would have puzzled an experienced accountant to reduce to order.

Paris was very busy plastering up her smaller wounds when I saw her once again. Though the great gaping gashes, the saddest blots upon her brilliant beauty, remain, weird and ghastly-looking, yet Paris is still, in spite of ruin and desolation of siege and fire, the very Queen of beautiful cities—more than doubled in extent since those long past times when it was home, and every street and turning perfectly familiar. New boulevards are everywhere, broad streets, handsome churches, gardens, 'squares.' You are bewildered; you seek to reach a well-remembered spot; you know it to be in the near neighbourhood; you strive for the most direct line; you reach a 'carrefour'; the thread of your course is broken, lost in a tangled skein of street architecture, and you probably decide to pursue your way confidently in the opposite direction; meet another 'carrefour,' and in the end wander back to the original starting point to begin once more, humbly asking directions at every turn and crossing.

Yet among all these changes some of the most striking points of city scenery remain unaltered. The old Boulevards have, if possible, improved by the growth of the trees, and another nearly unrivalled picture, the 'Cité' from the Pont des Arts, retains its crowning beauty by the almost miraculous preservation of the Sainte Chapelle. The floating baths, the old Samaritaine with the well-known palm-tree chimney, the fine old trees grouped near the Pont Royal, the swimming-baths and even the rows of washerwomen with their wooden bats, look now as they looked ten, twenty, thirty years ago; but a new element of animation and of very great public usefulness has been introduced on the river—the little steamers ('hirondelles') running between Bercy and St. Cloud. This water-way gives charming views of many buildings and parts of the city under quite a new aspect. Nôtre Dame and the grand ruin of the Hôtel de Ville are particularly fine, and it is well worth a trip up and down to look at Paris from the level of the Seine; the landing-stages are frequent, and the little boat calls at them about every five minutes: the charge for the run through the city is three-halfpence.

The method now adopted of transplanting trees of large growth is invaluable, not only on account of the new boulevards, which quickly become quite pleasant and shady, but also in replacing the trees destroyed by shot and shell ; some of these in the Rue Tronchet, as in the Champs Elysées and elsewhere, said to be quite newly-planted in place of those utterly destroyed during the late struggle, look as if they had had at least a ten years' growth on the spot.

The shops are full of pictures of the ravages of the civil war : Parisians, unwilling to lose the opportunity of sensation and profit combined, have photographed the magnificent desolation of their ruined monuments from every point of view, but in reality much of the destruction has been repaired with wonderful promptitude in most of the streets that had suffered severely, and the gaunt skeletons of such well-known massive blocks as still remain untouched appear the more startling by comparison. The ruins of the 'Grenier d'Abondance,' near the Bastille, give perhaps a stronger impression of wholesale destruction than the more important ruins ; from the immense extent of roofless walls and the almost countless rows of headless pillars, the place has the look of some vast ruined temple of the highest antiquity.

Nôtre Dame is uninjured, although three fires

were lighted in the interior; the 'tresor' also is in its place, in all the glittering splendour of broidered robes and jewelled cups, priceless crucifixes and saintly 'réliquaires.' And there, in a little closet beside them, as if in bitter mockery of the gorgeous accessories of their perilous elevation, hang the blood-stained garments, torn, and pierced, and soiled; the violet robe of the last unhappy victim—marked with bullet-holes in more than a dozen places—is covered, besides, with stains from the unhallowed ditch into which it had been thrust. One looks at the gold and glitter around with indifference—such things can be seen anywhere; but the poor torn and earth-stained relics of these martyrs fill you with deep reverence and almost overwhelming pity.

On the outside of Nôtre Dame some workmen, not long since, repairing the roof, found the body of a priest who had perished very miserably, fallen astride over one of the flying buttresses, probably in attempting to escape.

The destruction in parts of the immediate environs of Paris is more evident to a stranger than that in the city. At Issy, where the struggle between the Commune and the Versaillais was very sharp, these traces are terribly visible. Here, as elsewhere, people will tell you that they suffered little from the foreign enemy, that it was the Commune on the one hand, and the feverish ill-directed efforts of the French 'Génie' on the other, that caused all the ruin. The military engineers seem to have made widespread havoc in a wild attempt at defence, turning into dustheaps acres of smiling gardens, levelling villas and manufactories where (on the word of a competent authority) the destruction was as utterly uncalled for as it was unsparing. For instance, a tall chimney, the finest in all the country round, had been just completed at a vast expense; it had remained untouched during the siege and the fearful times of the Commune; nevertheless, it was doomed to destruction and blown up by the authorities after fighting had ceased, and the armistice waited but the last signature. In the same spirit of senseless waste they cut down the fine park of Issy, and were forced immediately afterwards to drag branches of trees to the spot to mask their batteries. The handsome stone bridge over the Seine at Choisy was blown up at a time when the water was so low as to allow the

Germans to pass on foot with the greatest ease; endless instances could be given of the needless destruction caused by the French themselves.

To speak further of France, where, on this occasion, I passed a month in that pretty fertile district between Paris and Étampes, which had remained happily an oasis of peace in the hands of the Germans, would be needless. I can record no novelty there. Time seemed to have passed by that favoured little spot, and to have forgotten, in the hurry of broad touches required of his pencil, by the wearing fret and onward strain of neighbouring cities, the delicate, tender little half-tints of the quiet, uneventful village life. I step back ten years with the loving welcome which brought me once again into the dear old-fashioned salon, with the bright polished floor, the downy bergères, the clock before the large chimney-glass, and the little chocolate service of Sèvres china on the marble console. I see through the open window the garden, a due proportion of bright flowers with vines and wall-fruit, melon-beds and vegetables in the background. Beyond that again, the shady wood and the spreading fir-tree, where, seated on an ancient bench, I presently hear how, as in old times, the good curé still continues to dine on stated days at the château, and at the two or three better houses of the village; how he plays his quiet rubber of bézique, and does his best to amuse an ancient 'demoiselle' 'who is getting very deaf now;' how old Père Rémy, the 'serpent' in the little village choir, wound his last blast upon that formidable instrument on the last fête-day, and how the girls of the 'Confrérie de la Vièrge' have ceased to wear their pretty little plaited caps, and are taking to chignons and imitation Parisian coiffures.

Then I hear many an anecdote of the German occupation (the Bavarians under General Von der Tann held the whole of this district): how, meeting with no resistance where resistance was indeed possible, they managed to live on quiet terms together; but poor old Étienne the gardener, in his casquette, blue apron and sabots, got a terrible fright one day as he peeped timidly over the wall from amongst the vines that he was trimming, at a spirited Uhlan capering about the road. 'Bon jour, papa,' said the warrior. 'Bon jour, monsieur,' said the poor old man, raising his casquette tremblingly, every gray hair standing erect with fright, and down came the sabots amongst the vines, and he did not feel very sure that the unlooked-for salute had not bewitched him, for 'the frémis (fourmies) have been very bad in the peaches ever since, comme qui dirait un sort, mamzelle.'

The Germans behaved very well in this part of the country, which they occupied undisturbed for several months ; during all this time no complaint was made of even a rudeness to a woman. The peasants worked in their fields and vineyards unmolested—sometimes, indeed, helped by their compulsory visitors ; their only troubles were the frequent requisitions for carts and cattle, which, after all, generally came back to their owners, or were paid for after the end of the war. But even these requisitions were sometimes resisted, as when three stout Uhlans entering one of the cottages while Geneviève was making her bread, she turned round upon them, heaving up an armful of the heavy dough, and declared she would throw it in their faces if they asked for anything more. The prospect was so alarming that the men of war instantly departed to seek for what they needed from some less determined housewife.

In C——'s house the ancient handmaid, the meekest and mildest of her sex, even ventured to revolt against some demand connected with her saucepans. 'Ah, my girl,' said the grim orderly, patting her encouragingly on the shoulder, 'never mind; patience! all this is misery for you and misery for us.'

Many officers and soldiers left their temporary homes with mutual feelings of good-will, and there is an amusing anecdote of a sick Bavarian, who, after living some time at Arpajon in M. B——'s little house, fell dangerously ill, and was removed to the ambulance in the château of our village, La Norville. It was mid-winter and bitterly cold; the poor soldier had brain-fever, and in his delirium he managed to escape in the night; barefooted, in his shirt, and holding a lighted candle in each hand, he made his way along the snow-covered road back into the little town, and knocked at M. B——'s door, 'because,' as he explained, 'he had forgotten to wish his kind host a happy New Year.' They wrapped him up in blankets and took him back; everyone thought his case hopeless, but strange to say he recovered from that time, and was soon quite well and strong again.

I could relate instances of many country houses well known to me occupied by the Germans, where, beyond the loss of a rug or a blanket, or perhaps some ink spilt on a cloth, there was absolutely no injury to complain of, and it was quite amusing to hear my friend E—— tell how she had left her country house in the sole care of the gardener, who was obliged to receive into it several cavalry officers; therefore, as everything there is very clean and well kept, he covered all the drawing-room chairs with newspapers to keep them nice for the return of 'madame,' and the conquerors actually submitted without remonstrance.

This same friend relates how, driving her little pony-carriage alone through the forest, strongly held by the Germans, she would often come suddenly upon pickets of solemn, motionless groups of mounted soldiers in the gloomiest paths of the sombre woods, who had no more thought of alarming the unprotected lady than the ancient trees under which they stood.

Other parts of France, in the hands of othe

regiments, met with rougher treatment; I can only speak of places that I know thoroughly and have since visited, and it seems that as tales of wrong and injury are always loudly proclaimed, it is but right to notice the countless instances in which conquerors holding resistless power over all around used it with so much gentleness and forbearance. Would the French, spreading over the Rhine provinces and entering 'à Berlin,' have acted with the like restraint?

Once more in England! carried onwards towards that overgrown metropolis, 'a province covered with houses'; onwards, past a wild stretch of gorse and bracken, a beautiful oasis, a rare glimpse of untouched nature; then on again, past villages with church tower or steeple rising from the clustering belt of trees; past fruitful orchards and graceful hop-gardens, homesteads with their 'oast' houses; a sweep of thyme-scented breezy downs; soft, dewy valleys between swelling wood-crowned hills; pasture-lands, with flocks and herds of well-kept cattle; sweet scenes of rural peace and industry and solid comfort infinitely soothing to tired wayfarers.

The journey, begun with the calm, indolent 'kief' of our slow progress up the Danube against the stream, had quickened slightly at Buda-Pesth; became brisk from Vienna, onwards; thrilled into interest in France and in Paris, rising from its ashes; and now, still flying onwards by rich pastures and wooded uplands and parks and stately mansions, we find that gradually the scenery becomes less rural, the stone and brick and mortar more encroaching. A haze hangs over the landscape; you are rushing towards it; the scattered cottages begin to cling together, in pairs at first, then in rows and terraces, until slowly, but surely, you become involved in a limitless maze of houses and streets, chimneys and steeples, railway arches and viaducts and tunnels, and rows of lamps, and vast illuminations of coloured signals, and rushing, palpitating, shrieking trains, and hurrying tides of human life. You are in London, where all the bewilderments of all the iron ways of Europe seem to culminate in the great rush and roar of the wonderful and fearful network of railway junctions, underground lines, and daylight station routes. It takes away your breath when you are first shot out—a floating speck—on this great ocean of indescribable vitality. Trains are rushing above, beside, beneath you all at once; there is more than one gloomy spot where, as you are whirled along beneath the living flood that surges heavily through the crowded streets, you are aware of a panting line of carriages tearing above the level of your progress, while at the same moment, beneath, in a deep gulf (a cutting in a yet lower and a darker depth), a railway train is passing; there, also, you are rushing into a tunnel, ending in some gleams of daylight of a sickly cavernous quality, from which you ascend, and thankfully breathe once more the outer air.

The past ten years have changed the whole face and aspect of this vast London; monuments of art, of science, of taste; charitable institutions, educational enterprises without number, have arisen during that short period; but while we rejoice in the results of these, many of them heroic, efforts for the benefit of the toiling masses, we must remember that *all* in our wonderful city is not matter for admiration and self-applause. A visitor to London is condemned to experience every sensation that the aspect of city life can produce, every sensation in excess. You wonder exceedingly ; you admire ; you shudder ; you rejoice ; you sympathize or you recoil, as scenes and objects incomparably beautiful or immeasurably sad pass before your view ; the extremes of luxurious ease and of heart-breaking misery and suffering are, it is well known, to be witnessed here in startling contrast, and yet what self-denying, what almost superhuman efforts of public and of private charity are ungrudgingly made to lighten this heavy burden of poverty and pain !

To see something of this sad aspect of suffering life, take an East London train, and soon you will be flying above and looking down into another world—a black, grimy, sordid, painful world. As far as the eye can pierce the dense cloud of smoke, gaunt chimneys rise above a vast ocean of shabby roofs and reeking factories ; streets and lanes and miserable alleys swarm with squalid life ;—a depressing, cheerless labyrinth, yet saved from the depth of dreariness by beautiful church spires that pierce the gloom, like fingers of hope pointing steadily upwards.

The smoky veil gradually lightens ; there is a

break in the dreary monotony of crooked chimney stacks and blackened tiles—a blighted, smoke-dried tree on a miserable patch of withered, trodden grass; a dusty bit of hedge; and now, the houses begin to separate, to show an open space, growing old broom-sticks and rusty iron; then a patch of clean grass; a garden with bright flowers; a breezy field with sunlight and flickering shadows; fresh hedgerows, some splendid trees, and you are once more in the open country—the placid, soothing English country; you breathe freely; and with deep thankfulness for the blessed sense of rest and peace in the calm repose of unspoiled Nature, you look back to the thick vapour hanging over London, with pity for its restless millions, with wonder and admiration for its gigantic enterprises, its strength of solid beauty, its vivifying streams of life ever pouring forth or gathering in its boundless wealth of thought, of knowledge, of science, of labour, of produce; and you feel that if Paris may be called the bright and dazzling Capital of Europe, London may be named, with even greater truth, the mighty, throbbing Heart of The World.

IN MID-WINTER, FROM VIENNA TO GALATZ.

FROM the beautiful station of the 'Nord Bahn,' at Vienna, its luxurious café and waiting-rooms, its marble columns, and rich, warm glow of colour and touches of gilded work, I turned to encounter, as best I might, the dreary discomfort of a solitary winter's journey through the frozen, half-barbarous countries which must be passed before reaching Galatz, on the south-eastern frontier of Moldavia.

At that time—1873—only one line of railway had been completed eastwards of Vienna, towards the Russian frontier; taking at first a north easterly direction, making an immense curve upwards through Austrian Poland, by Cracow and Lemberg, then downwards through Galicia to the Roumanian provinces.

I have taken a direct ticket by mail express as far as Suczava, on the Moldavian frontier; am directed to a 'Damen Coupé,' where two lady travellers are already installed; remark that the guard of the train is dressed as for a Siberian progress; and the train rolls slowly away from the Austrian capital.

The scenery on the east of Vienna is exceedingly flat and uninteresting, growing sombre as you pass into a region of fir plantations, where the trees stand dense, dark and straight, about as wearisome a picture as it is possible for trees to produce. Towards Prérau, the country becomes more attractive; an outline of distant mountains gradually rises on the left hand; there is a suggestion of a ruin on one lofty summit; the level country on either hand becomes more varied, sprinkled with villages and little groves of trees, until at Weïsskirchen you find a very pretty village with a majestic château standing in a beautiful park.

My two companions stopped here, and with a civil 'good-morning' left me the solitary occupant of the ladies' carriage. I was very sorry to lose them; they had talked to each other incessantly for more than five hours, the subject of their discourse being a certain Gräfinn, whose name never transpired ; but, although their conversation, quite unintelligible to me, was, consequently, not of absorbing interest, the carriage became very dreary when they descended, and the guard — muffled and sheepskinned, and smothered up into the likeness of an Esquimaux —shut me in alone.

Few ladies travel in mid-winter on these distant railway lines, and I saw small chance of companionship. It is certainly desirable to avoid the smoky horrors of the general carriage, where, through a blue fog, reeking with evil odours, you see nothing but huge masses of fur, that move every now and then, and give occasional signs of animation by spitting; but yet the melancholy dignity of a carriage to one's self, under the circumstances, is a choice of evils.

The route, quite new to me, passes over a tract of country subject to frightful snowstorms, and the consequent stoppage and blocking of trains; we had, as yet, since leaving Vienna, seen no trace of the winter clothing of the ground. The young corn was springing up, strong and green on either side, till, suddenly emerging from a tunnel, we shot into a land of snow ; gradually, as the afternoon wore into evening, the windows of the carriage became thickly frozen, and the outer world was an utter blank through the long, solitary night. The lamp in the roof, which had wavered and winked for some time in a friendly, companionable sort of way, got tired at length, spluttered a little, and subsided; thought better of it, made an effort, leapt up in a wild attempt to recover itself, but overdid it, and finally sank down exhausted, and expired, leaving a weird, unearthly sort of twilight; for a full moon existed somewhere in the heavens, and there was a pale gleaming from the snowy plains over which we were rolling so noiselessly.

The patterns on the frosty window-glass were beautiful; under more cheerful circumstances, one might have fancied waving trees and springlike vegetation; now, the fantastic lines form themselves persistently into sweeping snowdrifts, groups of bewildered travellers, dark, hurrying troops of wolves, and frozen inundated swamps.

There are occasional glimpses of human life as the flickering lamps of a station gleam through the obscurity, and, the door of the carriage being hastily opened, an uncouth mass of sheepskins pushes forward the heavy footwarmer, after which the guard, very friendly, and perhaps a little compassionate, looks in, pats the chauffrette, asks if it is 'gutt,' and shuts me up once more into my solitude, always leaving behind an impression of garlic and other strong restoratives.

Some time in the night a brighter gleam than usual announces an important station, my prison door is opened, and we are at Cracow. Several unmistakable Poles are lounging about, tall and straw-coloured; I mingle with my fellow-creatures for about a quarter of an hour in a 'restauration' heated by iron stoves to fever-heat, and obtain a basin of broth, for which I pay helplessly, by offering a coin more than four times the supposed amount, and taking up the change as if the currency were quite familiar; then back into my padded cell, and onward through all the weary hours until we stop to change trains at Lemberg, on the Russian frontier.

Two gentlemen enter the new railway-carriage, so muffled and hidden in furs that nothing can be distinguished of the individual; my opposite neighbour is lost in the stupendous collar and cuffs of a valuable dark fur ornamenting a formidable fur-lined cloak. An astrakan cap, pulled to the eyebrows ; a thick muffler concealing the lower part of the face ; great fur-lined gloves and an immensely thick railway-rug, completed a thoroughly arctic equipment. The sable trimmings and astrakan cap would formerly have denoted a 'Boyard' of the second class ; in the present day these distinctions have ceased.

It is really amazing to realize the amount of covering that travellers in these countries are able to carry on their persons. I had been much amused a few days previously in noting the contrast between an English gentleman and his opposite German neighbour, both preparing for some hours of night journey. The weather was far from cold, and the carriage, nearly full of passengers, close-shut, padded, and heated with the chauffrettes, might have been called oppressively warm : the Englishman simply exchanged his hat for a soft warm cap, spread a tartan shawl over his knees, and was satisfied ; the German, who chanced to occupy the warmest seat in the carriage, began by slowly inserting one leg, then the other, into a cloth tube lined with fur, with a great flap of fur which he pulled up to his chin; not content with this, he next dragged an enormous fur-lined coat all over him to his eyebrows, and finally extinguished himself under some thick head-wrappings, closing up all vestige of humanity from the snoring mass.

As the morning began to break, a bright ray stealing softly across the frozen window-pane spoke of brighter prospects, and it soon became possible to clear a small space, through which glimpses of the country might be obtained. Our route is taking a southerly direction; the snow is disappearing from the plains, although the rivers and gullies are still ice-locked, and the distant hills a glittering white.

We are in Galicia; the scenery increases in interest as we advance—slightly hilly, varied by woods; villages and homesteads rise amidst gardens and orchards; numerous streams crossed by little rustic bridges—a charmingly pastoral style of landscape to enjoy, at a distance, for the picturesque, low, whitewashed cottages, with their deep, overhanging brown thatch, may be otherwise than pleasant in the interior, the Polish peasantry not rejoicing in a reputation for cleanliness, but as subjects for sketching, their dwellings are perfect.

Galicia seems wonderfully fertile; comfortable villages and large farms are passed in quick succession, varied by woody uplands, patches of wild heathland, a sombre bit of forest here and there, and distant glimpses of the shadowy Carpathian range. After the dreary solitude of the frozen night journey, it is like a bright awakening from a painful dream.

One of my fellow-travellers also awakes, and, gradually emerging from his swathing wraps, proves to be a pleasant and gentlemanly native, sufficiently civilized to speak French, and I seize the opportunity of gaining some information about this interesting and comparatively little known corner of Europe.

Remarking on the great provision of wood stacked at the railway-stations, it appears that from Lemberg downwards, nearly to the Danube, the engines are heated with it; that the forests —fast disappearing—are not replanted, with the inevitable consequences of scarcity of winter fuel, in a climate where the winters are Siberian, and of summer droughts, in which the promising harvests of wheat and maize hopelessly perish. A new line of railway is, however, in contemplation. It will pass through the Carpathians, opening up a possibility of working with advantage the vast coal and salt mines and other mineral treasures that are known to abound in the neighbourhood of Okna.

The country is surprisingly well watered: our train is running continually over bridges. In the course of the night we twice cross the Dneister, and, some hours later, the Pruth, on a long picturesque bridge; the small streams and rivulets are countless. The line reaches also the Sereth, about half-way between Czernovitz and the frontier, crosses it two or three times, then follows the course of the stream till it flows into the Danube a little above Galatz.

Czernovitz, an important station which was reached soon after crossing the Pruth, looks more like an overgrown village than a town. The whitewashed, thatched, and rustic dwellings, standing in their gardens and orchards and farmyards, are scattered about over a great extent of land; a large church and some buildings, grouped on the summit of a low hill, seem to form the heart of the town, which clambers irregularly up the slope. Some pretty villas and substantial mansions on the further side show that the place contains wealthy families, although my fellow-traveller—who stopped here, and seemed to be an inhabitant—declared that the mixed population of Russians, Poles, and Jews formed a great hindrance to the prosperity of Czernovitz, which is very near to the Russian frontier line.

We roll on southwards, and with every turn of the wheel the scenery continues to improve in beauty and interest as we approach the foot of a branch of the Carpathians. Clearings in the thick forest growth are sprinkled with farms and deep-eaved cottages; a tangled gully runs up into a gorge with its rich, dense masses of primeval forest, and the dark, rounded summits carry the eye still further on to the vague, blue mountain outline, melting into the bluer sky. Then the mountains gradually recede and pass away, and with the fading light we reach Suczava, once the capital of Moldavia, and now a frontier town between the Austrian territory and Roumania.

Taking a fresh ticket for the Moldavian line, I find that florins and kreutzers have given place to francs and bàni, the currency, like all institutions in this part of Europe, being modelled on the French system.

We stop for a short while during the night at Romàn, where travellers for Jassy change trains. Nothing is visible of the town, one of those said to have been founded by Trajan when he planted his Roman colonies in Dacia, nor of the country through which we afterwards pass in the neighbourhood of Bakău. The train rolls on in a straight southerly direction, sometimes 'piano,' 'piano,' as it crosses great tracts of inundated land, or creeps over innumerable and very fragile-looking bridges. In some parts the line is slightly under water, and we can hear the sharp cracking of the ice beneath the wheels; then the steam is put on a little, and we roll more briskly, but never (although it is the mail-express) at a rate that could be considered in England as average railway speed.

There is not a vestige of a tunnel, scarcely even a cutting, through the whole length of the line, yet it had given infinite trouble to the engineers from the peculiar nature of the beds of the rivers, particularly of the Sereth; it had seemed almost impossible to find solid foundation for the bridges; the first built had been all swept away, and a great part of the line in Upper Moldavia has been entirely reconstructed.

At Barboshi, a little station near to the spot where the Sereth falls into the Danube, several passengers changed trains, and three ladies, whom I had met in the waiting-room at Suczava, and who knew that I was bound for Galatz, looked at me as they passed the carriage in which I sat quietly; they did not think themselves called upon to enlighten the stranger, the guard left everyone to themselves, and I presently found myself placidly making my way towards Bucharest. This was not quite in the right direction; there was no remedy, however, but to make a little impromptu excursion into Wallachia, and at the next station, Ibraïla, to take a ticket back to Barboshi.

The day has dawned as I wait for the Galatz train, and gaze idly from the door of the little station, upon a low hill or bluff of earth on the opposite side of the line: it would have had more interest had I then known that the green mound on the summit marks the site of a Roman fortress or encampment, known to the country people as 'Capi di Bové.' It is one of the innumerable traces of Roman occupation found in these parts, particularly along the course of the Danube above Galatz.

The train is drawing very near to that well-known commercial town; we are skirting a fine piece of water on the left, the lake Bratisch, backed by the low hills of Bessarabia, and soon the long earth cliff of Galatz begins to rise on the right hand of the line. I recognize the features of the town; there is the British Consulate, quite near to the station; the train slackens, stops, and the travellers disperse quickly, for this being a free port, there is no examination of luggage. The weather is very fine; I will walk up to the Consulate, so I pass along the broad road into the Strada Micaïau Bravul, and enter the spacious court, rather as if returning from a morning's stroll. Although unexpected at that time, I am welcomed with the warmest friendship. I came for a few days and I stayed a month; and although Galatz is generally reckoned one of the least interesting spots in this part of Europe, I found so much to engage attention in the manners and customs of the people, I heard so much of the beauty of the scenery in the mountainous districts of Roumania, of the curious cluster of women's convents, of the ruined churches and monasteries, of the antique usages especially preserved amongst the peasantry of the Carpathians, that before leaving I formed some plans for future excursions in this little-known corner of Eastern Europe.

How, many years later, these plans were realized amidst the wild and beautiful scenery of Upper Moldavia, where three English ladies, the first that had penetrated to these remote monasteries, found everywhere a gentle courtesy and a kindly welcome, has been related elsewhere, in the hope that others might one day also profit by their experiences of a simple and inexpensive holiday tour.*

* 'Untrodden Paths in Roumania,' Mrs. Walker.

THE BOSPHORUS, FROM ABOVE KURFESS.

To face p. 330.

*OUR BEAUTIFUL WATERWAY: BOSPHORUS
VIGNETTES.*

EACH year, with the return of the swallows, flights of tourists also arrive, eager to look at Constantinople, as they have already looked at (not *seen*) Egypt and Palestine, at a run, and as rapidly as possible. The greater number, 'personally conducted,' can do little more than skim the surface. Tired and bronzed and weather-beaten by desert travel; the head filled with confused remembrance of pyramids and picnics, of tossings on camel back and steamer, of grave and solemn feelings before the Holy Places, mixed with the miseries endured in the last hostelry, they climb the steep ascent to Pera, displaying with delightful unconcern the most impossible costumes, well suited, perhaps, to tent life and the ruins of Baalbec, but of startling eccentricity in the very modern and up-to-date High Street of our suburb.

But our travellers have no time to think of such a trifling matter. Must they not crowd into three or four days as many impressions as possible of ancient Byzantium and of modern Stamboul? Are there not the mosques, the hippodrome, antiquities and bazaars, the unrivalled circuit of ancient walls, and the last improvements of civilization, all to be raced over? They must see the Sultan go to his mosque; the dervishes who turn, and the dervishes who howl, at their religious exercises; and, not least, the veiled and elegant Turkish ladies, whose carriages animate the promenade. What an amount of labour to be got through in four days! Nothing but the broadest outlines of ideas can compass it, and our tourists, to gain an impression of the Bosphorus, invariably climb up to the deck of the steamer, from which the two shores can be seen at a glance: the European girdled by an unbroken range of palaces and yalis, of smiling villages and graceful pavilions; that of Asia, less thickly inhabited and more rural, offering many a view of wooded heights and shady glades, with vaporous mountain-summits that melt into the far distance of little known Anatolia.

The excursion, no doubt, is delightful; nevertheless, the traveller returns with a vague feeling of disappointment. This much-praised Bosphorus does not realize expectation: the hills lack grandeur, and the whole loses in comparison with so many other well-known sites. To appreciate the beauties of this celebrated waterway, they should be taken in detail, and are best seen, if possible, from a caïque, or steam-launch, or from the cabin of a steamer, almost on a level with the water, where, through the little windows on the shore side, you obtain a moving panorama of exquisite vignettes.

Should the excursion be made during the few days in early spring when the wild Judas trees glow like gigantic rose-bushes all over the rough ground above the belt of houses, those who are happy enough to have seen it will long remember the tender, fairy-like beauty of the picture. One of our former ambassadors returned here at the age of eighty-two, for the sole purpose of seeing once more the blossoming Judas trees of the Bosphorus.

The frame of our first picture is filled by the

gangway—a narrow plank with, or sometimes without, a handrail. A many-coloured, picturesque crowd is pushing forward to embark for the different stations on either shore, for this steamer is what is popularly called a 'crossing-boat' or 'zig-zag.' There are civilized people and barbarians; fine ladies in gauzy toilets and peasants in sheepskins; mollahs in green or white turbans, and dervishes in felt flower-pot hats; Turkish hanums in satin and diamonds, and beggars in dirt and rags. They press forward; they hurry; they swarm along the deck or upward to the benches under the awning; some ladies to a side-cabin reserved for Mussulman women; the greater number of the fair sex to the harem, divided from the deck by heavy curtains.

A sharp whistle; we are starting. With a harsh noise the gangway is drawn back, while the pedlars leap back on to the bridge over the narrow chasm; belated travellers hurrying down the rough steps gesticulate in vain; the most adventurous endeavour to get on to the boat, in defiance of shrieks and cries of prohibition. The machine beats its wings for some minutes, and we are off—very slowly at first, for the harbour is choked with craft of all kinds that seem to throw themselves purposely across our line of progress.

In the cabin, which can hold about eight people, we find a group that excites our curiosity—three men, partly crouched upon the cushions, dressed in beautiful silk caftans, interwoven with gold. They wear magnificent turbans, whose gold and brilliant colours shine through folds of delicate muslin; they have shed their slippers, which lie on the floor beneath; they speak in subdued tones, and roll their black velvet eyes with superb indifference on a scene which must be, to them, so novel, for we learn that they come from some wild country of Central Asia, and are accompanied by a palace agha, six feet high, black as a coal, and polite as a courtier; he does the honours of the boat in the shape of black coffee and cigarettes.

Beside the negro a little French governess is seated, on her road to her daily lessons. Picturesque scenery has lost all novelty for her, and she is knitting, to while away the time—striving, perhaps, to reckon how many years must be passed in this weary round of toil, before the bright time comes—if ever—when she may hope for rest, and the enjoyment of the beauties of this beautiful world.

A fat man seated near watches with foolish, sleepy eyes the nimble fingers of the poor girl; were he to express his thoughts, they would probably be: 'Amàn, Amàn? how dreadfully it tires me to see you working like that!' But he says nothing, and the bright needles continue their fencing exercise. The cafedji comes and goes: the inspector of tickets tears off a corner from a slip of coloured paper printed in four languages, and I turn once more to the moving panorama of the coast.

We have left behind Galata with its majestic tower; Pera, its Embassies and its many-tinted houses covering the slope of the hill; the fine mosque of Tophaneh, its gold-pointed minarets, and the long range of cannon foundries, which have lately considerably increased in extent and importance, thanks to the labour and intelligence of English workmen and overseers.

Above Tophaneh, houses in terraces, mosques, barracks, climb the steep hillside, until on the highest point, as if to complete this scene of life and actuality, the sombre forest of cypresses, the

'Great Burial Ground,' literally called 'The Great Field of the Dead,' cuts like a stern grim curtain upon the intense blue of the bright sky.

Beyond Fundukli begins the garland of palaces, yalis, kiosques and gardens, of cafés and kïefs, which lines the shore in an almost unbroken string till within view of the Black Sea.

At Cabatasch we draw up for a few minutes. In the foreground a little wooden châlet serves as waiting-room; beyond, an old arabesque fountain at the top of a flight of half-ruined steps; beside it a group of idlers slowly smoking narghiles in the shadow of a spreading plane-tree. They are talking, perhaps, of the good old times when tramways, carriages, and all the traffic that now covers them with dust, were unknown; when the 'Cabatasch,' a large mass of ancient masonry, might still be seen beside the rough landing-stage, or of other things connected with this spot, and with the little cemetery beside the road.

Off again. Our series of vignettes continues to unfold. Now it is the white mosque of Dolma Bagtché, with the imperial palace rather in the background, for our steamer is tracing a great curve in order to pass behind the Sultan's yacht, and the ironclads, all at anchor for the summer under the eyes of the Padischah.

The Palace of Dolma Bagtché is a beautiful building in white marble, wrought, sculptured, embellished to the utmost extent. Architects of severe taste lament over its mixed style; jokers compare it to a highly-ornamented wedding-cake; it may be so, but I doubt if a simpler, more correct edifice would produce the same magical effect, with the sparkle of its thousands of luminous points in the azure mirror that repeats them, as the water laps gently on the great marble landing-stairs. On the edge of the quay, as on the roof of the palace, a colony of white birds with pearl-gray wings and rose-coloured feet remains undisturbed by the great Imperial caïque, with its crimson-and-gold awning and fourteen pairs of oars, that balances softly before the principal entrance.

We have reached Beshiktash; we recognize the flotilla of caïques and its rustic cafés, with wide-spread coloured awnings and wandering garlands of vines below the tomb of the celebrated Barbarossa, High Admiral of Soleyman the Great, with the mosque and school of his foundation. The cupola of the tomb has lately lost the gilt anchor on the point which marked its especial character, and if care be not taken the building will ere long disappear from view, hidden in the maze of branches of the ancient trees by which it is surrounded.

We have just left a palace, and again it is a palace that fills our little frame. Tcheraghān, where no princely personage lives, or will probably ever live, is the most extensive, as it is the finest, of the modern palaces of the Bosphorus; in Moorish style, with a happy mixture of coloured marbles and of red and green pilasters ornamenting each window of the graceful façade. The palace of Tcheraghān was built by the Sultan Abdul Aziz; on the completion of the work he signified his intention of inspecting the building, and, entering the principal doorway, most unhappily stumbled on the threshold. This was an augury of such direful portent that the Sultan refused to set foot again in the beautiful but fateful palace; by a sad irony of fate, it was to this place that he was brought after his deposition, and it was here that he——died.

Behind the palace, beautiful gardens and park-like uplands roll their masses of rich foliage to the summit of the hill, with pavilions and kiosks half-buried in the dense leafage.

The rounded hillside has glided away; it is a rough bit of nature that now takes its place: a projecting bluff, half rock, half red-earth, a cascade of branches and wild creepers, a majestic cypress or two, some venerable sycamores, cupolas, wooden kiosks in decay, bits of old wall, rose-coloured once, now faded by sun and wind, a neglected corner of an ancient garden, happily free as yet from modern embellishments.

We stop; it is the 'scala' of Ortakeuy; the background of the picture is not interesting, but cries and strange sounds are heard from the gangway. An immense Angora sheep has to be got on board, and the owner is dragging it by its gilded horns; the beautiful silky fleece is speckled over with gold-leaf and rose-coloured spots, a bright ribbon is round its neck, and the broad brow displays a medal. The poor beast, a sadly unwilling traveller, is pulled in front, poked from behind; the captain gets impatient, the sailors scream and gesticulate, everyone offers advice, to which no one listens, and at length the creature is embarked, leaving the gangway free for other passengers. Here are two Sisters of Charity, with their snowy caps and gentle presence; an Albanian, his broad belt fitted with weapons, some young Greek girls, and lastly an exalted ecclesiastic of an Eastern Church, who advances with dignified calm, ignoring the general impatience.

We are rounding a projecting corner of one of the numerous curves that make the beauty and the charm of Bosphorus scenery, and the boat runs quite close in shore, almost touching the quay, in front of a vast wooden building, a palace, though not strictly imperial, belonging to A—— Sultana, aunt of the present Sultan, married to the Minister of Marine. The lady is strict in all matters of propriety, therefore the ground-floor windows are furnished with 'cafesses' (wooden gratings) of the severest pattern, not, as is customary, three parts up, but reaching quite to the top, so that the fair 'halaïks' have not the smallest chance of exhibiting even the tips of their slender henna-tipped fingers to the admiration of passing strangers. One may imagine, therefore, the agitation, the excitement, that reigned behind those jealous blinds, when it was announced in the harem that the six most beautiful girls belonging to the household were to be prepared to appear before the Sultan, to whom his sister had promised the choice of one of their number. The reason of the promise is thus related. A—— Sultana had an only and dearly-loved daughter, whom she wished to marry to a son-in-law of her own choice; the Padischah had other intentions, in the interest of a favourite courtier; there were many and long discussions between the brother and sister, and at length the lady, a woman of great determination, carried her point, but upon the condition that the Princess should present the Sultan with the most beautiful girl in her household.

The six fairest were chosen and taken to the palace by the chief Agha. Dressed alike in white satin, they formed such a fascinating group of beauties that the dazzled Sultan, unable to make a choice, declared that at least two of the number must remain. The Agha protested; the monarch was inflexible, and the unhappy guardian of the girls, incapable of bringing forward fresh arguments that might be sufficiently respectful, called in the Princess (in hiding behind a half-open door), and the discussions recommenced;

but this time the lady had to yield, and the Sultan, by way of consolation to those who had not been chosen, led them before some enormous coffers, telling them to take and carry away all that they could grasp. The girls plunged their hands, their arms, into a mass of diamonds, rubies, pearls, precious stones of all kinds, and could scarcely tear themselves at length from this almost fabulous wealth.

This story, if not strictly true in every detail, is at least 'ben trovato.' The conclusion is so thoroughly characteristic of the insensate luxury of the East—to amass fortunes in precious stones ; to shut them up in coffers from which they rarely see the light ; to keep vast riches lying useless and forgotten. Who knows the amount of these buried resources ? And the peasantry starve for lack of roads to utilize their harvests. Government clerks without regular payment live in misery or rob in order to live. The country is impoverished ; commerce is failing ; and all this time they say untold wealth, sufficient to reanimate business, to succour all this misery and want, remains buried in the forgotten coffers of more than one Imperial seraï.

Our steamer is crossing the Bosphorus to touch at Candilli, where the Sultana just mentioned has a summer palace—an imposing-looking building that crowns the high promontory; then, gliding past the ruins of the old castle of Anatoli Hissar, we reach some wildly picturesque, antique wooden houses on the edge of the water, and a small kiosk standing partly out in the stream on piles.

It consists of one large room beautifully decorated in the Persian style, which gives it the name, commonly used, of 'The Persian Kiosk,' but it is more properly called the Tulip Kiosk, on account of its origin and history. A certain Grand Vezir of Sultan Selim II., in order to ingratiate himself with his master, who was passionately fond of tulips, pretended that he also was smitten with tulipomania, and that he possessed some rare and unique bulbs, and he induced the Sultan to promise that he would himself see and judge of the beauty of the flowers described. Perhaps some question of self-interest made it highly desirable that the visit to the Grand Vezir, a very rare and unusual circumstance, should be duly noticed and commented on; at any rate, Ahmed Pasha had the kiosk rapidly built (being of wood, it could be done in a few days), the plots of ground on either side planted with rare bulbs in full bloom, and a broad band of frieze below the ceiling painted with a long row of the most beautiful and variegated amongst them.

The story, as I learnt it, has no sequel; whether the Pasha gained any advantage by his magical promptitude remains a mystery, but the kiosk is still there, with its exquisite interior decorations, and the frieze of tulips all in fairly good preservation. It now belongs, with the adjoining property, to the Scheïk of an order of Dervishes.

We cross the Bosphorus once more, for we are still in the 'zigzag' boat, to touch at Emirghian, where the fine range of Yalis lining the shore, and the magnificent gardens reaching to the summit of the high hill, are the property of the Khedive of Egypt; then, by one or two more crossings, by which many passengers are landed at the fashionable summer resorts of Therapia and Buyukdereh, that are dignified by a succession of 'Palaces' of the various great Embassies, we emerge from the seemingly endless panorama of brick and mortar, stone and marble, and rejoice in rugged hillsides, crags, and heather-covered slopes; the wide horizon of the Black Sea in front, the fort of Roumeli Kavak on our left, as we turn once more towards Asia, and stop at the last scala on the list of stations, Anatoli Kavak.

At Kavak there is 'païdos,' which means a pause for rest before starting on the return voyage. In the deep shadows of the beautiful bay, the quaint old galleon-shaped vessels from the Black Sea, with the high prow and carved and ornamental stern, ride at anchor; the furled sails, the masts, and ropes, relieved against the fresh green of mulberry and plane-tree, are repeated in the clear depth of the liquid mirror below.

In the deep shade, rustic shops in irregular line display bunches of candles, eggs in wire baskets, spades, ropes, sausages of dried mutton, sugar-plums, cheese and various sweet stuffs in rude glass bottles. A quiet group of venerable loungers seated on the low stools (iskemlé) nod their turbans as they sip coffee or smoke the peaceful narghile. The shadows are broken here and there by bright flickers of sunlight, or the gleam of a white minaret beyond the leafy boughs;

at the foot of the noble tree-trunks, with their spreading roots, the clear water ripples, in which myriads of tiny fish glance and dart and sparkle. Beyond the deep shadows, a broad warm light on boats and sails, through which a blue vapour rises from an ancient caïque that is undergoing the process of pitching; two old Turks in red jackets are looking on, and the heavy graceful masses of the great fishing nets stream and wave from the giant branches.

Near the rude landing-stage a display of melons and various fruits is protected at the back by a screen of old tawny-coloured matting, and behind this is a rustic coffee-shop, its rude balcony graced by a bright row of flowering balsams. Now and again a man in gay-coloured jacket and crimson fez will saunter across the gleam of sunlight, or a woman with trailing feradji and fluttering veil pass silently with her pitcher towards the well at the foot of the great plane-tree. . . . But the steamer is once more moving; we are leaving the shore of Asia, and as we steam out into the Bosphorus the grand masses of the ruined castle of Anatoli Kavak, sometimes called the Genoese Castle, with its long range of towers and walls following the dip of the valley and reaching to the shore, appears to rise slowly and majestically above the wilderness of foliage and the peaceful old-world Asiatic village on the shore.

We are crossing towards Europe ; on the right the broad horizon of the Black Sea looks to-day calm and innocent, its blue surface dotted with white sails against a bluer sky, and we have, in turning, a momentary glimpse of the rugged forms of the Cyanean rocks rising grim and gray near the foot of hills that are green with bilberry bushes, heather and wild lavender.

A little further on the picturesque group of ' dalyans ' (fishing huts), with their attendant boats and wide circle of nets, crowns a bewildering maze of poles and ropes and ladders. These dalyans are in some places merely represented by an immense inclined pole, as in the Bay of Beïkos ; it supports a man who, from that height, can see the shoals of fish hurrying on their travels towards the Sea of Marmora, and direct the operations of the fishermen below.

We touch at Roumeli Kavak, where some ruins of a castle crown the summit of the highest hill ; at Mezar Bournoa ; at Buyukdereh, and at

Therapia; then, at a sharp angle, pass over to Asia, below the Giant's Mountain and the marble palace of Beïkos, to pause in the beautiful green inlet of that most lovely spot, for the valley behind the palace, dear to innumerable parties of cricketers, is chiefly remembered by the artist for its stately and venerable trees, its soft turf, and the sylvan beauty of its days of unruffled solitude.

We are now rapidly passing down with the current, and wondering at the transformation that a few years have accomplished at Pasha Bagtché. Four villas standing in lovely gardens full of leafy shade are backed by hills clothed thickly with foliage, where, eight or ten years since, the whole space and rising ground was peeled and bare, and the beautiful groves and villas as yet unthought of.

But we are drawing near to a 'scala' where destruction in that same period shows in an ornamental balustrade, ruined, and forlornly crowning a flight of broken steps that lead to nothing but a mass of charred fragments ; all that now marks the site of the handsome yali of the celebrated statesman, Fuad Pasha. It was here that, long years ago, a brilliant fête was given in honour of the Sultan's birthday; it included a ball in the harem (between ladies only, as a matter of course), and the curious contrast—the struggle between the old style of dress and the endeavour to imitate French fashions—was a sight not easily forgotten. Two Egyptian Princesses—visitors—splendidly dressed in robes stiff with gold embroidery, sat in haughty indifference to the gay scene, smoking cigarettes in holders incrusted with jewels; the Buyuk Hanum (Mme. Fuad), in a costume of severe simplicity, looked as if she wore her dressing-gown, while a tiny niece—a child, yet already married—stood before her in a fashionable dress of rose-coloured satin and lace distended over a balloon-like crinoline. Crinoline, alas! had already invaded the harems, and as the younger women did not yet dare to cover the schalwars (wide trousers) with a fistan or skirt (strongly condemned by the stricter ladies as being a 'ghiaour' dress, and therefore highly objectionable), the effect of the upper part, without the accompanying flowing lines and folds, was, to say the least, extremely comical.

. . . The steamer is still hurrying onwards, with scream and whistle as we approach the various headlands and landing-stages, and we are passing the spot where, in a gale of wind, the prow of a vessel carried off the projecting portion of a house overhanging the water. It floated gaily down towards the Bay of Kurfess, a beautiful creek, opposite the 'yali' and grounds of the late Halim Pasha of Egypt at Balta Siman. I can never look upon that group of buildings without a saddened remembrance of the charming and graceful Circassian girl who had been carefully educated with the eldest daughter of the Pasha, and whom, after that daughter's death, he married—Vidjany Hanum, best known as the Princess Halim. She was a lovely woman, when, not expecting visits of ceremony, she reclined on the broad divan in a flowing morning gown of some soft creamy material, her rich, dark hair confined by one wide band of diamonds. When receiving State visitors she wore costumes sent from Paris, and lost as far as could be possible the greater part of her graceful charm; but that she was in every respect worthy of esteem and regard, no better testimony in her favour could be given than the high appreciation expressed by our ever-lamented Ambassadress, Lady Elliot.

Vidjany Hanum died a victim to the disease so often fatal to Circassian women—consumption, but one or two letters written to me in perfect French are amongst the cherished relics of days and friends for ever passed away from earth.

I pause at Candilli on the Asiatic shore; it is the narrowest part of the strait, so narrow that the bark of dogs and music in the water-side cafés can be distinctly heard from either Continent; it is also the most lovely and the most interesting portion of our 'Beautiful Waterway,' offering the strangest contrasts between the old and the new customs, manners, ways of life, dying prejudices and daring innovations.

From a window overhanging the stream one sees on the right hand the small marble palace of Gueuk Sou, shining and carved and fretted; beyond it, a meadow bordered by a fine grove of trees; then a space of rather marshy, reed-grown land, on which an insignificant board marks the spot where the great telegraph lines to India and the far East cross between Europe and Asia; beyond this a tiny stream (the Sweet Waters) flows into the Bosphorus at the foot of a gaunt gray ruin, a massive square keep, some round towers, and a broken line of crenellated walls. They take us back to the times when Tamerlane had not as yet overrun with his wild hordes this beautiful Asiatic shore, for this Castle of Anatoli was built, or at least founded, by Badjazet Yilderim in the height of his power and magnificence, about fifty years before the opposite castle of Roumeli was erected as an outwork of the enclosing circle that reduced the power of the expiring Byzantine Empire to the space within the walls of the city which bore, and still bears, the name of its founder, Constantine.

What an exquisitely varied scene is this waterway between the two Hissars! what movement! what animation! what wonderful variety! from the slender caïque, the little skiff, the 'sandal,' the 'mahone,' the busy steam-launch, the Bosphorus steamers, to the stately three- and sometimes four-masted vessels that carry passengers and goods between England, France, Austria and Italy and the ports of the Black Sea. They keep as far as possible the middle of the stream, going upwards light in the water, with much of the red keel visible; returning laden with grain, or it may be with petroleum from Bacu and Batoum.

Close in shore a lively commerce is being carried on, for in summer-time the Bosphorus becomes a sort of water-market; every imaginable article of daily use floats and dances on the wavelets under the windows of the 'yalis,' and it is quite easy to conclude important bargains from a first-floor balcony.

A fisherman pulls up slowly and stops; the fresh fish is leaping in the bottom of his boat; an animated discussion is carried on; he asks too much, and as he pulls away, a common-looking, shabby craft drifts round the projecting corner of the house, and a wailing, dolorous lament proclaims that a beggar has chartered a caïque to pursue his doleful calling. The next craft means tangible business; it is a boat laden with porcelain, glass and crockery; it is followed by heaps of vegetables, baskets of fruit, mounds of melons. A pretty sight is a boat-load of flowers in pots; then comes into view a haberdasher's display of printed stuffs, muslins, laces, calicoes; the butcher and the baker also find this water-way the most convenient road to custom; and a barrel-organ in solitary state enlivens the scene from its own private caïque. A little later in the afternoon ice-creams ('caïmakli dondurma') begin to float upwards towards the fashionable promenade of the Sweet Waters, and many boat-loads of holiday-makers are hastening to land in the shadow of the grove of trees that partly conceals a beautiful fountain, a well-known landmark, or, pushing on still further, enter the little river beneath the grim old ruined castle. There are many parties of Turkish ladies, some in the brilliant and delicate colours that produce such combinations of tints with the pearly blue of the water and the soft green of the grass and foliage; others in the now fashionable shrouding of black silk from head to foot. As to this funereal garment is often added a half-veil of black gauze, or, worse still, a dark muslin with tawny, leprous-looking spots, one may well feel that in truth 'the old order changeth,' and that the much-vaunted brilliancy of Eastern costume is here at least rapidly vanishing.

The boats, however, are gaily painted—white, with a bright blue or green band; they skim the water like swallows, all streaming towards the outlet of the little river under the gray ruins. They are bound for the gay gathering near the wooden bridge of Gueuk Sou, and the graceful seagulls, scarcely disturbed by the glancing caïques, are hovering, circling, dipping their white and pearl-gray wings, adding an exquisite grace and beauty to this busy, animated scene.

We look across the Strait towards the hill of Roumeli Hissar, that, to the old inhabitant, offers more startling contrasts, more clear evidence of change, than any spot on these historic shores. The extreme point, rising sharply from the water, where the current is so strong (they call it the Devil's Current) that boats are often towed along it for some distance, is, in the lower part, a Mussulman cemetery, and in the memory of the writer that hillside was thickly grown with cypress-trees. It was very beautiful, casting deep reflections in the water. A massive round tower rose majestically above the dark foliage. To-day the trees have mostly disappeared, and such as remain look scanty and meagre. The blame is sometimes laid to the charge of a little téké of Dervishes that exists in the corner of the cemetery, in the shadow of a tower on the quay. To wilfully cut down a living cypress in a cemetery is forbidden, but it is not difficult to wound the tree so that it withers and threatens to fall; then it is

ROUMELI HISSAR.

legitimate prey, and cypress wood, so easily embarked and sent to Stamboul, is much esteemed there for trunks and boxes, as a preservative against moth; so the little old téké still flourishes, as the charm and beauty of the spot is passing away.

Looking further up the hillside, we see the battlemented summit of another of the four towers, that, with their connecting walls, compose the circuit of this old fortress. Beside that tower, nestled against it, stands a picturesque, old-fashioned, red wooden house, the property and summer residence of one whose name was widely known and honoured for his high character of incorruptible integrity, his great learning, and his splendid library—Ahmed Vefyk Pasha—and those who knew him in his family circle will never cease to regret the kind and bright welcome in that home that, through long years, had never failed. It was a patriarchal household: the aged and honoured mother of the Pasha, the one wife and their family of five, two sons and three daughters. The world is poorer for the loss of that learned and kindly man.

But a startling contrast awaits us on a still

higher platform, above and beyond the topmost tower of the old fortress, in a stately pile of buildings that had no existence when first I knew the red wooden konak. It is the great American College—a splendid institution, undertaken and carried on by a staff of professors of the highest order, where the most modern of scientific inventions, the most startling discoveries of this end of the century, are known and expounded almost before the world in general has even heard of them; where lecture-hall, library, museum, every appliance for study and also for healthy recreation, combined with a perfectly-organized system of careful training and kindly discipline, have already sent into the world men who are capable of making their mark in their generation, and of raising the standard of principle and conduct among the smaller States of Eastern Europe.

Must we look higher still? Yes, to the very summit of the highest hill; but what we there look upon must take the mind back a few centuries, for the rather uninteresting dwelling that crosses the point where the grove of trees stands dark against the golden glow of the sunset is a 'chiflik,' or farm-house, at the same time that it is the téké of a celebrated order of Dervishes—the Bektashies. A remote ancestor of the family, Hadji Bektash, in the time of Orkan, about five centuries ago, blessed and gave the name to the newly-formed body of troops, calling them 'Yeni Chéry' (the new troops), which name we have converted into janissaries. Hadji Bektash and his descendants became attached to this body of troops, and followed Mehemet Ghazi to the conquest of Constantinople, when the Bektash Dervishes fixed their téké on this hilltop, and were there buried in a little cemetery under the grove of dark trees.

The office is hereditary; each succeeding Scheïk of these Dervishes has been laid to rest in that spot, and the present dignitary, when his time shall come, will be succeeded by his son Mahmoud.

The cemetery, in which the Dervishes' burial-ground is enclosed within rough palings, is known as 'The Cemetery of the Faithful,' as it is supposed that those who died in the castle before the siege of Constantinople, or who fell during that siege, were buried here. It is a most lovely spot, and offers, as many think, the finest panoramic views on the Bosphorus. The lowering sun's rays are streaming through the gnarled branches of the grove, touching here a tuft of flowering cistus, there a mossy, irregular gravestone; they pass across the pale mists in the deep valley, to touch with bright dashes of vivid green the stately crown of a splendid stone-pine; to glance upon the tall cypress; then—with a golden glow upon the ancient battlemented towers—strike sparks of fire from the palaces and houses of Candilli on the Asiatic shore, and fade into the pearly mists of distance, through which, far away on the right of the picture, the mosques and minarets of Stamboul gleam as in a fairy vision.

And thus from this point of exquisite beauty we look—perhaps our last—upon this fair land of 'lost opportunities'; a land so blessed by the Almighty Giver of all beautiful things that rejoice the heart of man; so blighted, so cursed, alas! by the shuddering horror that throws a pall in these dying years of our century over what might have been—over what may yet become—almost an earthly Paradise.

NOTE ON ANATOLI KAVAK.

THE following notes and information on the subject of Anatoli Kavak are entirely due to the late learned Dr. van Millingen, and were kindly communicated to the author by his son, Mr. Julius van Millingen.

Kavak.—On the summit of the hill there formerly stood one of the most renowned temples of antiquity—that of the twelve gods of the air and the sea, generally known as the temple of Jupiter Ourius (the fortune-giver). According to tradition, Thrisus, the son of Nephile and Adamante, offered sacrifice on this spot on his return from the Argonautic expedition, which occurred about twelve hundred years before our era.

The place was considered sacred, and was called 'The Jeron.' Thither mariners used to resort to appease the gods with purifications, and make them propitious with gifts and sacrifices before undertaking a voyage into the Euxine.

Jupiter, Neptune, and Diana were the divinities principally worshipped; but in the temple ultimately raised stood the statues of twelve divinities; that of Jupiter, in gold, was the most conspicuous.

The desire to possess a spot commanding such influence and wealth naturally led to many a conflict. The Chalcedonians, on several occasions, wrested it from the Byzantines, returning it only on payment of large sums of money. It was also taken by Prusius, King of Bithynia, but finally restored to the Byzantines, who at length fortified it, and stretched a chain to the Thracian shore, in order to prevent ships from passing without paying toll.

The temple is supposed to have been converted by Constantine into a Christian church; but, according to others, the materials were employed by Justinian in building a church to St. Pantaleïmon, on a rocky eminence above Kavak. It had doubtless repeatedly been despoiled of its wealth by the inroads of the Persians, the Goths, the Gauls, and others.

According to Herodotus, when Darius had reached the Bosphorus and his artizans were throwing a bridge between the two Hissars, he sailed up the Straits and visited the sacred spot on the summit of the Kavak hill, whence he gazed on the Euxine extended before him. The Euxine was then considered the most wonderful of seas, and Darius, who intended sending his fleet thence into the Danube, may not improbably have attempted to propitiate the ruling divinities with sacrifices.

The Persians were probably masters of the spot till 479 B.C. The Scythians who pillaged the Bosphorus between the years 350 and 400 B.C. were undoubtedly unwelcome visitors to the place, which also must have suffered when, in 378, Brennus crossed the Bosphorus with 10,000 Gauls. The following inscription, found on a slab at Kadikeuy, and now in the British Museum, would indicate that it was under the rule of Philo Antipater :

'The navigator who invokes Jupiter Ourius in behalf of a fortunate voyage among the steep Cyanean rocks, filled with numerous shoals scattered here and there, may have a prosperous voyage, if he beforehand sacrifices to the god whose statue has been placed here by Philo Antipater, so as to be a help and a good augury to navigators.'

Falling into the hands of the Rōmans, it was seized by Mithridates.

Gibbon relates that in 196 B.C. the Goths entered the Bosphorus, and so great was the terror inspired by these barbarians that the garrison of Chalcedon, sent up to the heights of Kavak, although far more numerous than the invaders, fled at their approach.

Kavak was attacked by the Russians in 865 and in 941. The castle on its heights was taken by the Genoese; it was besieged by Haroun-al-Rashid, and finally taken by the Turks under Bayezid.

This castle was built after the time of Constantine. The gateway between the two towers of the citadel belongs to another epoch, and was, perhaps, removed from the former temple of Jupiter Ourius. Several shafts of columns, capitals, friezes, and marble slabs may be seen in the walls, and, doubtless, belonged to the building, remains of which are found in the cemetery under the grove of trees a few hundred yards distant.

The castle was called the Jeron Polichnion (the Holy Lighthouse); from this we would infer that it was also used as a beacon.

On the wall over the main entrance we find a cross surmounting the crescent, with the letters 'ΦC. XC. ΨC. ΠC.' which, recalling the name, allude to the words of the Greek Litany, 'Light of Christ, shine over all.'

On the sides of the towers facing the gate may be seen two crosses opposite to each other, and two on the sides facing the cemetery; one of these is half hidden by the ivy.

On the walls inside the citadel are two other crosses—one a double cross, with the letters opposite each arm, IC XC NH KC ('Jesus Christ, the Lord Conqueror'). The other cross has a carved arch and two columns around it, with the following letters, Δ.Π.M.C., probably forming the initials of the emperor under whose reign the castle was built or restored.

Santi speaks of a Latin inscription existing in his day to the effect that 'Lercarius, a citizen of Genoa, repaired, at his own expense, and extended to the sea, the fortifications of the sacred promontory which had been destroyed by the injuries of time'; but there is no trace of it to be seen to-day. As already mentioned, the castle was held for a time by the Genoese ; it still bears their name, and a number of Venetian and foreign coins are dug up by the gardeners at the foot of the hill.

The citadel had two gates, one facing the south, the other the east, as already mentioned ; this latter had a portcullis, of which the traces may still be seen. During the last siege by the Turks, a wall was built before the gate, and the space between filled up with rubbish, so as to hide it completely. The number of arrow-heads found close against the walls of the towers would lead one to suppose that this was done by the besieged, to prevent the gate from being forced open.

It was by a mere accident that, in 1863, Dr. Millingen discovered the gate behind a breach in the wall. The British Museum having failed to obtain permission to make excavations, Dr. Millingen applied to the Turkish Government, and had the rubbish near the gate cleared away ; but not finding any other objects but skulls and arrow-heads, the Turks gave up the undertaking as unremunerative.

I think there is little doubt that the temple of Jupiter Ourius stood in the cemetery called, owing to the graves of Mussulmans who fell during the siege of the castle, 'Sheïtler,' or Place of Martyrs. The spot is strewn with carved stones, which the Turks made use of as tombstones. The size of some of these is so large as to negative the supposition that they may have been brought there for that purpose.

The position is admirably suited for a temple such as history records, and it needs only an enterprising Schliemann, and an unsuspicious government, to ensure the discovery of many hidden treasures.

Among the archæological remains found on the spot we may allude to :

(1) A basso-relievo, found by some fishermen in the sea,

below the grove, and purchased by Dr. Millingen; it is now in the British Museum. It represents two female figures, seated, measuring a rod with the span; two other figures, a male and a female, are standing beside them, and evidently awaiting the decision that will be given by Rhabdomancy. (2) A slab with the letters ΑΝΑΖΠΣΙ in high relief. (3) A large slab found at Anatoli Kavak in 1877, with a long inscription in Greek.

THE END.

BILLING AND SONS, PRINTERS, GUILDFORD.
J. D. & Co.

www.ingramcontent.com/pod-product-compliance
Lightning Source LLC
Chambersburg PA
CBHW022104290426
44112CB00008B/546